The Institute of Biology's
Studies in Biology no. 45

Biology and the Food Industry

H. R. Barnell

M.A., Ph.D.(Cantab.), B.Sc.(Lond.), F.I.Biol., F.I.F.S.T.
former Chief Scientific Adviser (Food),
Ministry of Agriculture, Fisheries and Food

SEC
Edward Arnold

on
15.12.93

© Elsie Eileen Barnell 1974

First published 1974
by Edward Arnold (Publishers) Limited,
25 Hill Street, London W1X 8LL

Reprinted 1976
Reprinted 1977

Boards edition ISBN: 0 7131 2436 9
Paper edition ISBN: 0 7131 2437 7

Printed in Great Britain by
The Camelot Press Ltd, Southampton

General Preface to the Series

It is no longer possible for one textbook to cover the whole field of Biology and to remain sufficiently up-to-date. At the same time teachers and students at school, college or university need to keep abreast of recent trends and know where the most significant developments are taking place. To meet the need for this progressive approach the Institute of Biology has for some years sponsored this series of booklets dealing with subjects specially selected by a panel of editors. The enthusiastic acceptance of the series by teachers and students at school, college and university shows the usefulness of the books in providing a clear and up-to-date coverage of topics, particularly in areas of research and changing views.

Among features of the series are the attention given to methods, the inclusion of a selected list of books for further reading and, wherever possible, suggestions for practical work.

Readers' comments will be welcomed by the Education Officer of the Institute.

1973   The Institute of Biology,
                                        41 Queens Gate
                                        London, SW7 5HU

Preface

This booklet covers in outline some of the constituent parts of the food industry particularly of the United Kingdom, emphasizing the influence on it of the biological nature of its raw materials. Food production is omitted except where its problems influence the treatments used in the processing, preservation and distributive phases of the industry.

In the writing of this booklet many books and original articles have been consulted and much assistance and advice has been given by former colleagues of the author. Amongst the many who have helped are the following: Mr. P. E. Martin and Mrs. C. M. Jones (Food Science Advice Division, M.A.F.F.), Dr. D. Axford (British Flourmilling and Baking Research Association), Professor E. J. Rolfe (National College of Food Technology), Professor J. B. M. Coppock (Spillers Ltd.) and Mr. J. F. Hearne (Food Science Advice Division, M.A.F.F.).

The several companies and others who have supplied illustrative material are mentioned in the captions to the illustrations.

Finally, but not least, the impeccable typing assistance given by Mrs. Barbara Brownlie must be gratefully acknowledged.

Folkestone,   H. R. B.
1973

Contents

1 The Food Industry

The food industry is not one coherent industry but a collection of diverse industries each dependent on processing the produce of the land or sea. If it is accepted that the food processing industry covers all treatments received by a food from its origin to the point in space and time when it is consumed then very little of the food we eat receives no processing. Most foods, except fruits, are not fully edible (i.e. palatable as well as nutritious) in the form in which they are produced and need at least a heat treatment to transform them from potentially edible to edible materials.

A considerable proportion of the food supplies are normally available (particularly for the industrialized minority of the world's population) from sources distant from the consuming populations. They must therefore be moved and stored in some form which allows them to arrive on the table in a condition both palatable and nutritionally sound.

Processing to make potential foods edible and to preserve foods obtained in times of plenty for use in times of shortage has been practised since before the beginning of recorded history. The difference between early methods—heat treatments, withdrawal of water, pickling and curing—and modern methods is that we now have more controllable treatments, more knowledge of their effects (chemical, physical and biological) and more certainty of producing foods of consistent quality and palatability with known nutrient composition.

1.1 Treatments used in the industry

The main treatments used in the food industry are mechanical, physical, chemical and biological or combinations of these. They were summarized by Barnell and Hollingsworth (1956) as follows:

1.1.1 Mechanical

(i) Grinding or pulverizing. (ii) Separation of some parts of original material. (iii) (a) Mixing of nutrients, (b) Addition of colouring matter (may also be chemical) and flavours.

1.1.2 Physical and chemical

(iv) Application or removal of heat. (v) Application or removal of water, reduction of water activity by addition of sugar or salt. (vi) The application or removal of air or the use of either oxidizing or reducing agents. (vii) Emulsification. (viii) Addition of chemical preservatives, including smoking. (ix) Application of gamma or beta rays. (x) Control of pH.

1.1.3 Biological

(xi) Fermentations.

It should be added that the exclusion of light is also of importance particularly in relation to the stability of vitamin A, vitamin C, riboflavin and nicotinic acid and the development of rancidity in some fats.

Very few food industries are limited to the use of a single treatment but usually one is dominant and is supported by one or more others.

In the milling of grains, for example, the dominant process is grinding and pulverizing but there are associated treatments for cleaning the grain, for separating the ground fractions and for treating the flour with various additives including nutrients.

The application of heat is used in canning, pasteurizing, baking or cooking; while the removal of heat is the basis of chilling, freezing and quick-freezing.

The addition of water is necessary in canning, fermentation and pickling. The withdrawal of water is the basis for concentrating, condensing, dehydro-freezing and for all forms of drying: sun drying, hot air drying and freeze drying.

Many manufactured food products are packed, either in a vacuum or in an inert gas (usually nitrogen or carbon dioxide), to prevent loss of vitamins or the oxidation of fats, pigments and flavour components. The addition of air or inert gas is necessary to give the requisite texture, e.g. to certain fats and ice cream. Oxidizing and reducing agents are used in many processes, e.g. oxidizing agents accelerate the maturation of flour for breadmaking and the reduction of unsaturated fatty acids in vegetable oils by hydrogen in the presence of a catalyst (hardening) is an essential stage for margarine manufacture.

Many raw materials are colloidal in nature, e.g. milk is an emulsion of fat in aqueous phase, and many processes involve dealing with or producing colloidal systems, e.g. foams (air in liquid), e.g. salad cream.

Ionizing radiations (gamma and beta rays) can be used for sterilization, pasteurization and specialized applications such as disinfestation of grain, elimination of parasites in meats or the suppression of sprouting in potatoes and onions.

The addition of sugar, salt, smoke or chemical preservatives is the basis of traditional methods of preservation, but is also used in modified form for modern products. The addition of colouring and flavouring substances is designed to improve the appearance and palatability of foods and hence their attractiveness.

Each branch of the food industry needs to be treated as both an art and a technology based on scientific knowledge. It attempts to produce food products of uniform quality from raw materials showing the variability natural to living plants and animals. For this reason food processors have tended to extend their influence further and further back in the food chain not only to guarantee continuing supplies but also to ensure that their supplies remain as uniform as possible and give end-products of as nearly as possible unvarying good qualities. This going back further in the food chain also enables the processors to obtain varieties of the food which are most amenable to the processing operation or to give the greatest yield, e.g. the cell walls of cling-stone peaches contain a greater insoluble pectic fraction than do free-stone varieties, and the high retention of insoluble pectins in ripe cling-stone peaches explains the firm texture of these varieties as compared with the soft ragged texture of ripe free-stone varieties and thus their preference for canning.

2 Raw Materials

Food production depends on photosynthesis by green plants. The energy for the synthesis of sugars is supplied by the sun's radiation while the carbon dioxide in the atmosphere provides the carbon, and water provides the hydrogen and oxygen. Energy for the synthesis of other compounds, e.g. proteins, is provided within the plant by respiration, sugars, in particular, providing the substrates (Figs. 2.1 and 2.2).

The green plant is the mainstay of the organic world. Animals and colourless plants depend on the products previously formed by green plants. There are a few bacteria, however, which produce carbohydrates and proteins by chemo-synthesis, e.g. nitrifying bacteria, iron bacteria and colourless sulphur bacteria.

Although the production of food by the green plant is fundamentally important to life it appears to be inefficient in its basic function of carbon fixation. The potentially useful fraction of the incident radiation from the sun is about 12%. Allowance for respiration reduces this figure to 8–10% of the possible efficiency of growth in terms of dry matter production. But even good farming gives an efficiency of only about 1%. This gap between the theoretical and the practical utilization of the incident light is as yet not fully understood.

It is interesting, perhaps, to compare this apparently poor performance of agriculture in utilizing the earth's incident radiation with man's effort in generating electricity in power stations using coal as fuel. If the national average is taken then little more than one-fifth of the heat energy in the coal consumed in the production of electricity is contained in the electricity delivered to the domestic consumer's premises. The remaining four-fifths is accounted for by losses in generation and transmission.

Green plants tend to give one the impression of flowering plants but the phytoplankton of the sea and fresh waters together with other forms of lowly plant life which contain chlorophyll or similar pigments are also capable of photosynthesis. The phytoplankton in the sea provide the beginning of the marine food chains culminating in fish, crustacea and other sea foods.

The starting-point of a food industry is the produce of the relevant branch of agriculture or fisheries. The final qualities of a food offered to the consumer depend not only on the skills of the factory staff and the care of distributors and marketeers but also to a large extent on the producers and their interlocking knowledge of varieties, plant and animal husbandry, catching techniques for fish, storage and transport of produce. Any of these

NITROGEN CYCLE

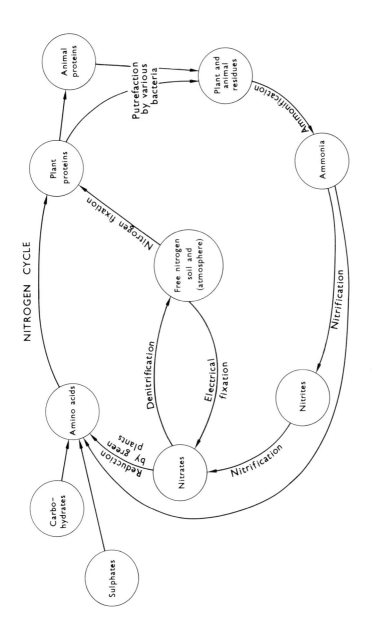

Fig. 2-1 The nitrogen cycle

CARBON CYCLE

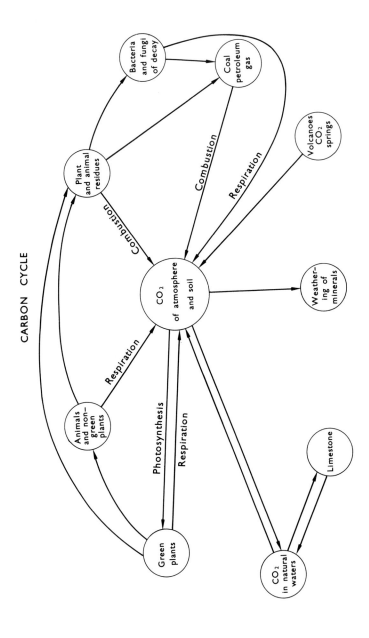

Fig. 2-2 The carbon cycle

individual procedures can and do influence the final qualities of a processed food.

The primary materials for the food industry may be simply tabulated:

Foods of plant origin	1. Cereals: wheat, maize, rice, barley, oats, rye, etc.
	2. Sugar: raw sugar from cane or beet
	3. Vegetables: peas, beans, potatoes, leafy vegetables, beetroot, etc.
	4. Fruits: a wide variety
Foods of animal origin	5. Meats: beef, lamb, pork, poultry
	6. Dairy products: milk, eggs, cheese
	7. Fish, etc.
Foods of animal or plant origin	8. Fats and oils

On purely economic grounds the factories processing foods tend to be sited near or in the areas of production but there are sound scientific reasons for this, apart from the evident economic ones. Any primary produce on harvesting, begins to undergo biochemical changes which are usually deleterious. It is also liable to fungal or insect infestation. Accordingly the shorter the interval between harvesting and processing the better the product is likely to be. Quick frozen peas, for example, are normally harvested, processed and frozen in less than twenty-four hours. Fish processing is done mainly at the main fishery ports but a certain amount is done at sea.

With the concentration and expansion of industrial capacity the direct relationship between producers and processors is increasing. It is the processor now who largely determines what is grown, how it is stored pending delivery, and probably contracts for the method and date of delivery before the crop is grown. In many instances the operation from planting to processing is planned with the detail of a military exercise. In other instances such as the milling of wheat and baking there is more latitude but there are problems of storage in pest-free conditions for both the wheat and the flour. The centralization of bakeries raises problems of maintaining freshness in wrapped or unwrapped, sliced or whole loaves in the retail shops.

3 Food Preservation

The most evident forms of food deterioration are biological being caused mainly by bacteria, yeasts and other fungi. Accordingly, the preservation of food depends on finding means of combating the activities of such organisms.

Early man lived from hand to mouth hunting, fishing and collecting wild fruits and nuts, but sooner or later in pre-historical days he attempted to keep stocks of food and to carry foods from place to place. It is likely that he early identified foods that were relatively resistant to spoilage, and that this played a part in his choice of crops, e.g. wheat, barley and pulses. With no knowledge of the nature of food spoilage the first attempts at food preservation began with the drying of these crops. This consisted in using the sun's heat to remove water from the grain or other crop until the levels remaining were too low to support the growth and reproduction of microbial organisms.

For thousands of years meat products such as biltong and pemmican have been made from sun-dried thin meat slices, fish have been split and dried in the sun and wind and grain dried in various ways. Later but still primitive methods of preservation include salting and smoking. Salting is similar to drying in that it deprives the potential spoilage organisms of available water both by the osmotic effect of the surface salt solution and by the partial drying which usually accompanies the process. Smoking, most usually associated with fish, includes some measure of drying but also adds chemicals which act as antibiotics and antioxidants (these include phenolic compounds which would not be acceptable today as deliberate additives).

Other relatively ancient methods of preservation were pickling and fermenting. In these methods the pH of the foods was changed so that the growth of micro-organisms stopped altogether or spoilage organisms were inhibited while acceptable organisms were encouraged. Examples of pickled foods include meats, fish and vegetables. The making of cheeses depends on the fermenting of milk by various organisms.

The delay of spoilage by freezing or low temperatures was early known in cold climates and now with the vast strides made in mechanical refrigeration is perhaps the most widely used method of preservation in the developed countries of the world.

Canning can hardly be regarded as an ancient method since the earliest experiments were attempted in the early nineteenth century by Appert in France and Saddington in England. Appert packed foods into stout glass bottles which were hermetically closed before heating. He bottled meat, fruit, vegetables and milk. His products were tested by the French Navy in 1806 and he was awarded a prize of 12 000 francs. Saddington in 1807 preserved fruit in wide-mouthed jars with loosely fitting stoppers. These were placed in a bath and heated to 72°–77 °C for about an hour after which they were filled to the brim with hot water and tightly closed. The Society of Arts awarded him a prize of five guineas for his invention.

The significance of the heat treatment in these bottling methods did not become apparent until Pasteur's work on micro-organisms in the sixties of the last century led to the appreciation of the part played by these organisms in food spoilage. The development of canning proceeded directly from these early experiments.

This brief treatment of early methods of food preservation leads naturally to the study of modern methods. All methods fall into one or more of the basic treatments, heat transfer, mass transfer or addition of substances with special properties such as preservatives or antioxidants. Although drying and dehydration are not such large industries today as canning and freezing they perhaps deserve precedence over other methods because of their ancient history.

3.1   Drying and dehydration

Drying is of great antiquity as a form of preservation. Dried foods thousands of years old have been found and Marco Polo reported that the Tartars dried milk in goatskin bottles over their camp fires. Today very simple methods of hot air drying are frequently used for the drying of herbs. Captain Cook in 1772 took a 'portable soup' with him on his voyage round the world which consisted of a glue-like material obtained by boiling meat until much of the water had evaporated. Dried vegetables, all rather unpalatable, were used in British ships' stores during the nineteenth century.

Dehydration, as opposed to simple drying, has been described as a process in which water is removed from food, under controlled conditions, to give a product, which, by the addition of water, will regain its original form and remain palatable and nutritious. This definition is still a useful one but limited. Dehydration is now used to provide a range of products which do not necessarily reconstitute into forms identical with the raw materials from which they have been produced.

With increasing knowledge of the biochemistry and microbiology of the raw materials and advances in engineering techniques, dehydration has developed considerably in the past forty to fifty years. Also in common with other processes of food preservation, especially canning and freezing, much progress has been made in producing varieties and strains of foods suitable for dehydration and in improving conditions and speed of transport of the raw material to the factory and its preparation for drying. These treatments include cleaning, cutting into dice or strips and scalding or blanching. The treatment of blanching or scalding consists of passing the material, particularly vegetables, through steam or hot water to de-activate the enzymes* which otherwise cause colour and flavour changes during processing and storage of the product. It also considerably reduces the bacterial load carried by the material which can be of importance if there is a delay between reconstitution and consumption. Modern methods of blanching have reduced the time required to a minimum and so reduced leaching losses (soluble solids; sugars, amino acids, etc.) and flavour deterioration.

There are at least eight methods of dehydration in use and there is considerable variation within each.

3.1.1   Hot air dehydration. Piece form foods

It is important in hot air dehydration that the hottest air (85°–101 °C) should be in contact with the wettest material and the temperature should be reduced as the material dries. At 40–50% water content vegetables such as cabbage easily turn brown under the influence of heat (complicated reactions known collectively as 'the browning reaction'). At low water content high temperatures can cause 'case hardening' when some products become hard and brittle and reconstitute with difficulty. This is believed to be partly due to salt migration during drying towards the surface causing some denaturation of proteins, e.g. skin formation on hot milk.

There are numerous kinds of hot air driers but in all of them the material is placed on meshed or perforated trays or belts or sprayed into a tank. The trays may be in cabinets or tunnels and the air passed over or through them. In tunnels the hot air usually passes first in parallel with the movement of trolleys containing the trays and then, if there is a second 'dry tunnel', the air is passed counter to the movement of the trolleys. There is usually some recirculation of the used air in addition to the intake of fresh.

In fluidized-bed drying the material is kept suspended and moving by a hot air blast. This provides relatively efficient heat and mass transfer and hence a short drying time.

3.1.2   Liquid foods and pastes

(i) SPRAY-DRYING. Spray-dried eggs and also milk were developed and much used during the last war. Considerable improvements in the products have since been made. The liquid is injected through a fine nozzle

---

* Enzymes: organic catalysts of complicated nature which regulate most of the metabolic processes in living tissues. An enzyme normally consists of a protein (the enzyme proper) and a co-enzyme, various activators may be necessary for efficient functioning. Enzymes are found in the protoplasm of cells and are responsible for both anabolic (building) and katabolic (degrading) processes. For a full description of their nature and functions any modern text book on biochemistry may be consulted. See also another book in this series *The Structure and Function of Enzymes* by Colin H. Wynn.

into a large inverted conical tank where, in the form of droplets, it meets uprising hot air. The suspended material speedily dries and falls as a powder. Pasteurization of liquid egg before drying is difficult but is necessary if any salmonellae are present and removal of the sugars in the egg white by treatment with glucose oxididase provides a more stable product. Spray-dried skimmed milk is difficult to reconstitute but may be converted into a 'soluble' powder by treating it with steam to form porous aggregates containing 10–20% moisture, then drying these to less than 6% moisture. Complex physical and chemical changes are involved in this apparently simple process. Spray-drying is widely used now for many products, e.g. coffee, tea and fruit juices.

(ii) DRUM DRYING. In this method, used before and during the last war particularly for milk and still used, the liquid is run as a thin film over a heated roller. It dries almost immediately and is scraped off as the roller turns. There is some loss of solubility in the milk but it is digestible and used for baby feeding.

The process, with variations, is used in the production of potato flakes and 'instant' breakfast cereals.

(iii) VACUUM-DRYING. Vacuum drying appears attractive because of the low temperature that can be used so ensuring less loss of quality during drying. However, it is not easy to obtain a high rate of heat transfer to the material and so the process is slow and not generally suitable for food dehydration.

(iv) FREEZE-DRYING. Freeze-drying has long been known and used for pharmaceutical and biological materials. A popular illustration of the nature of the process is the drying of wet laundry in the open on a frosty day. The water in the clothes freezes making them stiff, then sublimes (i.e. passes from the solid to the vapour state without passing through a liquid phase) and the washing becomes dry without the ice having melted.

If the freeze-drying process is successfully carried out the final product is so little altered that the addition of water in many cases at once restores it to its original state, viruses and microbes resume living processes, sperm can be used for artificial insemination and human tissues retain their specific antigenic properties.

The simplest type of freeze-drying equipment consists of a cabinet connected to a vacuum and condensing system. The frozen material is loaded on trays which are placed on shelves in the cabinet. These shelves are heated either by circulating hot water or electrically, and heat transfer to the material is largely by conduction from the shelf to the lower side of a tray, and by radiation from the lower side of a shelf to the upper side of a tray. The amount of radiant heat transferred in this way is relatively small compared with the conducted heat, so pieces of food material tend to curl upwards from the supporting tray, giving point contact only, and so reduced conducted heat. This combined with cushioning effect of vapour escaping from the lower side of the material tends to give inefficient heat transfer and so results in slow drying times.

These deficiencies were to a considerable extent overcome by the Accelerated Freeze Drying Method invented and developed at the Research Establishment of the Ministry of Agriculture, Fisheries and Food in Aberdeen (1961). This process arose from the Vacuum Contact Plate equipment and method devised at the Atlas Company, Copenhagen about the end of the 1939–45 war.

The method, very simply, consists of maintaining a high vacuum in a chamber and providing a high capacity evacuating system capable of removing the large amounts of water vapour at peak periods of sublimation. The frozen food (in some cases freezing of the food may be effected by evaporative cooling in the vacuum cabinet) is sandwiched between shelves of expanded metal (aluminium or stainless steel) resting on large metal trays. These trays are loaded between the hollow shelves in the vacuum chamber. The shelves are automatically closed together to make first contact and then pressure is applied (up to 0.5 kg/cm²) to the expanded metal sheets and so on to the material. The trays are heated by circulating hot water through the hollow shelves. This method provides intimate contact between the heated shelves and the material through the expanded metal sheets and the latter ensures free pathways for the emerging vapour to escape into the chamber from which it is then removed by the steam ejectors or vacuum pumps.

This method was an appreciable practical advance and introduced a new range of foods which could be dried to easily reconstituted acceptable products which, if suitably stored in an inert atmosphere or in vacuum packs, could be kept for long periods. However, it still had its problems due in part to the inherent variability of the raw materials; meat, fish, vegetables, fruits, etc., and also it was not a cheap process. It can be said, however, that it has provided a stimulus for commercial development of the various forms of freeze drying now being increasingly used in the food industry.

An example of a modern development, continuous freeze drying is shown in Fig. 3–1.

(v) MISCELLANEOUS DRYING METHODS. Three further types of dehydration all in use today may be mentioned. These are Belt-Trough-Drying, Puff-Drying and Foam-Mat-Drying. In *belt-trough-drying* hot air is blown upwards through a wire mesh conveyor belt moving in a trough. The fresh material, in particulate form, is fed on to the trough at one end and uniform drying is attained by tumbling action in the trough. High initial air temperatures (e.g. 150 °C) may be used but local overheating is prevented by the continuous tumbling of the material. A modern American technique which gives an open porous texture to the dried product is *puff-drying*. This is used mainly for vegetables which are first hot air dried to 40–50% moisture content and then placed in a chamber in which the pressure is raised to 2–4 kg/cm². On suddenly releasing the pressure by exposure to

Fig. 3–1 Prototype of world's first continuous freeze-drying equipment at Parma, Italy. Jointly developed and patented by H. J. Heinz Co. Ltd. and Rossi and Cotelli. Has a wet input capacity of 2 tons (2.0321 tonnes) per 24 hours and has been used to dry vegetables, fruits and cheese. (Photograph by courtesy of H. J. Heinz Ltd.)

the atmosphere the vegetables are inflated to a puffed form in which they are further dried. Because of the porous structure thus produced the final drying stage is short and the dried product is readily reconstituted. A method also giving a porous structure, *foam-mat-drying*, has been developed recently in the U.S.A. In this method foam stabilizing agents such as soya protein, albumen, sucrose, fatty acid esters and glyceryl monostearate, are added to liquids or semi-liquids and the mixture aerated and stirred or otherwise turned into a foam. Conventional air drying of foam mats on trays is rapid since the water readily evaporates from the liquid films surrounding the foam bubbles. Owing to the open porous structure of the product reconstitution is practically immediate. Applications include fruit juices (previously concentrated), potato, baby foods, fruit purées, egg and whole milk.

Brief mention may be made of the microbiology of dehydrated foods. The temperatures used in dehydration are not high enough to kill more than a proportion of the organisms on the raw materials. All methods aim to use the lowest temperatures compatible with an economic speed of drying to produce material of good flavour and texture when reconstituted. However, the dried material when packed has a sufficiently low moisture content to inhibit bacterial growth. This inhibition persists so long as the container is water impermeable or until sufficient moisture has entered to raise the moisture content of the dehydrated food above the critical levels. These are about 15% for bacteria and 12% for moulds in dehydrated vegetables. In packs impervious to vapour and air the total count of viable organisms in the foods decreases during storage.

The general micro flora of dehydrated foods is varied. The counts on the products may be kept low by close attention to hygiene at all stages. But even so the food is not sterile and there is a possibility of bacterial growth once the food has been placed in water for reconstitution. With most modern products only a brief period is required for reconstitution so they are particularly safe in this respect. Subsequent to reconstitution the foods are as perishable as fresh foods.

3.2 Pasteurization and canning

Canning has developed into probably the largest of the food preservation industries. Its products are the stablest and still have advantages over new forms such as quick-frozen in that cans or tins require, on the whole, no more specialized storage facilities than dry warehousing and, for transport, dry cargo space.

In the bottling experiments of Nicholas Appert in the early nineteenth century the well filled sealed bottles were heated in boiling water and then cooled. He did not understand the effect of this heat treatment and subscribed to the view of the time that contact with air as such was the cause of putrefaction. It was not until after the middle of the century that

Louis Pasteur worked on the inhibition of the souring of wine and beer by heating to 50°–60 °C for a few minutes and related the effect to the destruction of living contaminants (micro-organisms). It is thus appropriate that this heat treatment was called 'pasteurization'.

In the later years of the nineteenth century it was found that the souring of milk could be delayed by a similar heat treatment. As a result, dairies, particularly those in the larger towns of Europe and America, adopted pasteurization to prolong the time that milk could be stored without becoming sour. As further work was done on methods of controlling the time and temperature of treatments and the effects of so doing, it emerged that not only was it possible to destroy the organisms responsible for souring but also certain pathogenic organisms which might be present, particularly—*Mycobacterium tuberculosis.*

This outcome was gradually realized to be of great significance by public health authorities, and the introduction of pasteurized milk has greatly reduced the incidence of tuberculosis of bovine origin. The term, pasteurization, is more frequently used now to define processes designed to reduce the number of pathogens in a food to a safe limit. In this sense it has been adopted for suitable heat treatments of ice-cream and bulked liquid whole egg where the prevention of souring or other spoilage is not the main objective.

Modern canning is a complicated technology with a considerable background of physical and biological science. Its objective is the production of long keeping palatable safe food products which can stand up to almost any conditions of transport and storage. To achieve this end, heat treatments range from relatively light time-temperature applications for products such as canned beer and carbonated drinks, which are virtually pasteurized products, to massive treatments for non-acid packs such as meats, fish and most vegetables in which the aim is the complete destruction of all organisms within the can. Complete destruction cannot be achieved without the ruining, by over-heating, of the food in the cans but 'commercial sterilization' in which the count of spores of the most dangerous pathogen, *Clostridium botulinum,* is reduced in number by a factor of 10^{12}, is generally accepted by the industry as providing an adequate margin of safety. Simultaneously spoilage organisms are reduced to negligible numbers. The effectiveness of this practical definition of sterility is shown by the fact that confirmed botulism has not occurred for more than 30 years as a result of food canned in the United Kingdom, and a spoiled can of food is a rare occurrence.

The background of knowledge on which modern canning procedures are based is essentially biological in respect of causal organisms but physical in respect to heat transfer and conduction. Before a food can be processed successfully it is necessary to know the type of contaminating micro-organisms when the can is filled, the numbers of these organisms present, the influence of particular time-temperature treatments on them and the influence on these treatments of the nature (pH, salinity, etc.) of the foods and any surrounding medium. Also it is necessary to know the effects of the heat treatments on the foods themselves which can only stand a certain amount of cooking without undesirable changes of texture and flavour.

The microbiological flora on or in a foodstuff is large and varied but usually characteristic of the foods and their origins and, unless hygiene is very strict, of the processing factories as well. A potential source of contamination for meats is the abattoir in which the animals are slaughtered and butchered.

The art of canning consists in achieving the most appropriate time-temperature combinations to give the optimum quality of product while being adequate (with a safety margin) to inactivate the pathogenic and spoilage organisms initially present.

This art has been developed by applying engineering knowledge to accelerate heat transfer into the can so that processing time can be reduced without reducing the effectiveness of the treatment and resulting in an improved quality in the product.

After air exhaustion either by steam heat or pumps the closed cans are placed in autoclaves or 'steam pressure cookers' where the temperature is raised to the previously calculated level and retained for the required time. This is followed by cooling in water which must be bacteriologically clean as it may enter minute pinholes in the seams or lid closures and contaminate the contents (outbreaks of typhoid have been traced to this cause).

More rapid heat penetration can be obtained with certain packs if a rotating cooker is used. This end over end agitation causes mixing of the contents by the movement of the head-space gas in the can. Times have been reduced by as much as two-thirds by the use of rotating cookers.

Other forms of cooker are also in use, e.g. the hydrostatic cooker (Fig. 3–2) where the cans descend through a water column sustained by the pressure in a steam chamber; after the steam chamber the cans pass through a water seal and up another column of water, and are then air and water cooled. This is a continuous process in which the cans do not undergo any sudden changes of applied pressure.

With increasing supplies of natural gas there has been additional interest in 'flame sterilizing' in which direct heating of cans by gas flames is used. This process is in operation in Australia for dairy beverages and other applications such as the pasteurization and evaporation of fruit juices and tomato products appear promising.

3.2.1   Pasteurization and sterilization of milk

Pasteurization is a simple and efficient method of making milk safe to drink. All common pathogens likely to occur in milk are destroyed by a relatively mild heat treatment. The most resistant pathogen which may be

Fig. 3–2 Cans coming out of a hydrostatic sterilizer. This vertical tower is 19.812 m high and will sterilize 50 000 0.04536 kg cans at one time. (Photograph by courtesy of H. J. Heinz Co. Ltd.)

present is the tubercle bacillus which is killed by either of the two pres- ·
cribed treatments:

(i) THE HOLDER PROCESS in which the milk is heated to a temperature
between 62.8 °C and 65.6 °C for at least 30 minutes and then cooled
immediately to less than 10 °C.

(ii) THE HIGH TEMPERATURE SHORT TIME (HTST) process in which the
milk is heated to at least 71.7 °C for a minimum period of 15 seconds
followed by immediate cooling to below 10 °C.

The changes which give rise to the browning in milk have a $Q_{10\,°C}$
value of 3.1 whilst the destruction of spores of the various micro-organisms
likely to be found in milk has a $Q_{10\,°C}$ value of 11 to approximately 30
$(Q_{10} = \text{Rate at } (t + 10)°C/\text{Rate at } t°C)$. It is therefore apparent that a rise
in sterilizing temperature will lead to a greatly reduced contact time and a
substantial reduction in browning. This is the basis of the ultra high
temperature (UHT) for the sterilization of milk developed by the National
Institute for Research in Dairying in cooperation with the dairying industry.
A minimum operating temperature of 135 °C is used, held for a very short
period of time—sufficient to give a survival rate not exceeding 1 spore in
5675 litres of treated milk.

The sterile milk is sealed under aseptic conditions into sterilized
containers. This long-keeping milk has a flavour similar to pasteurized
milk rather than the cooked taste of long heat treated sterilized milk.

A similar process for other products, aseptic canning, is coming into use
in the United Kingdom. A canned custard produced by a UHT method is
being marketed. The custard is said to be heated to a high temperature for
a few seconds only and then cooled before filling into a heat sterilized can.
The filling and sealing take place under superheated steam in a sealed
chamber. A more natural flavour is claimed for the product compared with
conventional heat treatments.

3.3 The container

The almost universal container for heat sterilized products is the tin-
plated steel can, the tin in modern production being added by electro-
plating. This gives a thinner and more even deposition of tin than the cold
rolling method. With acid packs (most fruits) a lacquer on the tin-plate is
used to prevent action between the acid and the steel exposed through
minute holes in the tin-plate, giving 'hydrogen-swells'. These do not
indicate any danger to health but have the same appearance as cans which
have been 'blown' by the activity of spoilage organisms, some of which have
highly heat resistant spores. Such 'blown' cans are regarded as indicating a
possible inadequate heat treatment and result in the rejection of the product
so treated. Lacquered cans are also used for meat and fish products to
prevent sulphide staining.

The spores of the various types of the bacterium *Clostridium botulinum* are widely distributed in soils and so likely to contaminate the raw materials of canning. The environment in the can is anaerobic and if the pack is also of high pH the conditions are suitable for germination and multiplication of *Cl. botulinum*. But the spores do not germinate because the heat treatments are designed to destroy spores of organisms more heat resistant than those of *Cl. botulinum*. Other pathogens which may be present in the can contents are more sensitive to heat than *Cl. botulinum*.

Should there be a possibility of spores germinating owing to less intense heat-treatments, a method of inhibiting proliferation would be the inclusion in the can of antibiotics. The use of one, nisin, has been permitted under Food and Drugs Acts regulations in a very restricted manner.

3·4   Use of an antibiotic, nisin, in food preservation

The use of antibiotics for other than medical purposes is not encouraged in the U.K. and in fact all but a few of the known ones are banned for non-medical uses. Of these few, one, nisin, is used in canning and in some processed cheeses and cheese spreads; two others, chlortetracycline and oxytetracycline, are used in ice to retard the growth of bacteria in wet fish.

The use of nisin in food preservation is relatively recent, it being first considered for this use in about 1955 but then discarded as a possible therapeutic antibiotic. It has very low toxicity and is produced by the lactic acid bacteria naturally present in raw milk. It has relatively speedily become a recognized food preservative.

The first applications were with processed cheeses and some types of natural cheeses. The treatment of natural cheeses is difficult but that of processed cheeses and cheese spreads relatively simple and this use of nisin has developed appreciably during the past few years.

The application of nisin to canning is more recent and still somewhat tentative. It has developed with increasing understanding of its possibilities and limitations and also as food regulations permit. It is used:

(a) for the control of existing spoilage problems
(b) to permit in certain instances a reduction of heat processing conditions giving an improved product
(c) for the preservation of new products, e.g. heat sensitive foods not readily amenable to traditional canning methods.

At this point it must be emphasized that the use of nisin in low acid (neutral or high pH) canned foods can only be considered when a sufficient heat treatment is given to destroy *Cl. botulinum*.

Nisin is currently being used commercially in some canned vegetables, soups, tomato products, meat and fish pastes, flavoured milks and canned milk puddings.

3.5 Chilling and freezing of foods

The use of low temperatures for food preservation is of long standing; frozen meat cargoes reached the U.K. in the latter part of the nineteenth century and refrigerated ships carried bananas from Jamaica to Bristol in 1901. The aim in lowering the temperature is to slow down enzymic and other chemical reactions both in the food and in the accompanying flora of micro-organisms. With many foods this reduction or inhibition of the multiplication and activity of the micro-organisms is the more important effect.

It is common practice to divide micro-organisms into three classes: thermophiles, mesophiles and psychrophiles, depending upon their temperature ranges for growth. Although there are, as yet, no clear-cut definitions of these classes the following broad limits can be given for food spoilage organisms:

Organisms	Temperature range
psychrophiles	below freezing to about 30 °C optimum 25 °C (approx.)
mesophiles	10 °C to about 45 °C optimum 35 °C (approx.)
thermophiles	30 °C to high upper limit optima 50–60 °C

Mesophiles growing at temperatures well below their optima may multiply at a greater rate than a psychrophile having its optimum at the same temperature. Mesophiles having a temperature range extending well into the psychrophilic zone are of particular importance in food preservation. The term 'psychrotrophic' has recently been proposed for all organisms capable of growing at temperatures near 0 °C (STOKES, 1968).

The activities of micro-organisms are usually responsible for the putrefaction or deterioration of animal products and of fish and fish products but with fruits and vegetables the course is more frequently a continuation of their own metabolic activities. These activities may be slowed by exposure to low temperatures but the processes are not necessarily retarded in unison and abnormal conditions may result, e.g. browning in apples, 'chilled' effects in bananas. These abnormalities are physiological disorders resulting from diversions from the usual ripening or other sequence in the food material affecting, perhaps, the permeability of cells and their contents leading to a breakdown in their organization. A somewhat similar condition is observed in senescent tissues such as old leaves or rotting fruits.

3.5.1 Responses to low temperatures

It is clear that preservation by low temperatures is not simply a matter of lowering the temperature or even freezing and finding that each and every foodstuff will keep longer. Plants vary widely in their resistance to low and freezing temperatures and studies of their 'winter hardiness' have shown differences in the manner in which they may react to low temperatures. These include quick responses in the starch-sugar relation, the sugar concentration rising rapidly under low temperature conditions, and changes in the viscosity of the cell colloids resulting in greater water retention power. The changes decrease the water vapour pressure within the plant's atmosphere and so lower or eliminate the dehydration caused by evaporation of water from inside to the frost or cold dry air outside. So with fruits and vegetables the responses of each must be studied individually and allowance made for variations within a variety.

Frozen plant tissues are liable to suffer a loss of turgor and the loss of much free liquid on thawing. Secondary results of this free movement of water through the tissues are an increase in enzyme activity and an increase in susceptibility to the attack of micro-organisms. It is for this reason that vegetables are blanched (scalded) for a short period in steam or hot water before freezing.

In the freezing of meat, fish and poultry the effects are generally similar since they are all essentially muscular tissues but there are differences of detail between them. It is desirable in general for rigor mortis to be established before the flesh is frozen and at as low a temperature as possible without actually freezing. This is to reduce the tendency of the muscle to shorten and so become tough. It is a fairly recent discovery (LOCKER & HAGYARD, 1963; MARCH & LECT, 1966; DAVEY & GILBERT, 1967; DAVEY, KULLEL & GILBERT, 1967) that muscle which shortens during rigor becomes tougher than that which remains at its resting length. This is thought to be due to the overlapping of the actin and myosin filaments resulting in tighter bonding between them.

Rigor mortis is due to the decreasing of the amount of adenosine triphosphate (ATP) in the muscle. ATP is the immediate source of energy for muscle contraction. The ultimate source is glycogen and in the breakdown of this lactic acid is produced, the total amount produced depending on the initial amount of glycogen. The concentration of lactic acid determines the pH of the flesh, affects the growth of micro-organisms and affects the structure and the water holding properties of the meat. There are, however, marked differences between different kinds of flesh in the changes that take place during storage and thawing.

3.5.2 Mechanism of freezing

Various techniques have been developed in the quick freezing industry but the principles and operations are similar.

Freezing involves several stages:

(a) precooling from ambient temperatures
(b) supercooling

(c) freezing

(d) cooling to storage temperature.

These stages are illustrated in Fig. 3–3.

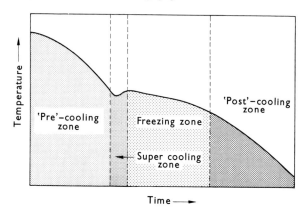

Typical temperature–time freezing curve

Fig. 3–3   Typical temperature-time freezing curve

(a) PRECOOLING. During the precooling stage the temperature of the material is lowered from air temperature to its freezing point. The time taken for this to happen depends on the overall heat transfer coefficient, the area exposed, thickness and the temperature differential. The overall heat transfer coefficient is a function of the *thermal conductivity of the food*, the physical properties of any packaging around it and the external heat transfer coefficient. This external heat transfer coefficient depends on the method of freezing which may be air-blast, plate contact or immersion in a liquid.

(b) SUPERCOOLING. This is a complicated process which varies in extent from one foodstuff to another and between varieties. It is important in connection with the course of ice crystallization and is affected by the rate of freezing.

(c) FREEZING. During this stage heat is removed during ice formation with relatively little change of temperature until the material appears frozen. It is during this stage that irreversible cellular and structural change may take place giving poor quality and storage characteristics. There is always a residue of unfrozen water in frozen foods the amount of which depends on the temperature.

(d) COOLING TO STORAGE TEMPERATURES. This stage is relatively quick as ice has a higher thermal conductivity and only half the specific heat of water. The rate of cooling has little or no effect on the quality of the product.

3.5.3   Freezing rate and quality

Modern methods of freezing enable the freezing zone to be passed through relatively quickly; thirty minutes is generally regarded as the upper limit. Slow freezing leads to loss of quality particularly in plant products.

The explanation for this loss of quality has, for a long time, been that slow freezing tended to cause the formation of large ice crystals, which disrupted delicate tissues. Quick-freezing results in the formation of small ice crystals which cause less damage. It is now thought that the effects of quick-freezing are not quite so simple as this; the position of the crystals within the tissue is regarded as of main importance. In slow freezing relatively large crystals are produced in extra cellular areas, in quick-freezing a *continuous* ice pattern is formed in both intra and extra cellular spaces.

3.5.4   Methods of freezing

The main methods used commercially are air-blast and plate freezing which are self-explanatory. Specialised literature should be consulted for details of installations and their operation.

As with dehydration a fluidizing process has been developed in recent years. The particulate material is partially suspended by a blast of cold air and the fluidized mass flows under gravity giving a continuous process.

Immersion freezing using liquid nitrogen, carbon dioxide or Freon 12 (a refrigerant, dichlorodifluoromethane) permits very rapid freezing but is expensive and must be regarded as still in the developmental stage. It is used for poultry.

3.6   Food irradiation

The use of ionizing radiations for treating foods has long been recognized. A French patent was taken out in 1930 for the use of X-rays to prolong the storage life of foods. Much work has been done, particularly in the U.S.A. and the U.K. during the past twenty-five years on the use of various types of irradiation, effects on the nutritional values of the treated foods, the possible production of toxic substances including carcinogens, chemical mutagens and induced radioactivity.

The interesting situation has developed, because of all the scientific knowledge that has been accumulated, of an industry being controlled in the U.K. by regulation before it has become established here. The use of ionizing radiations for the treatment of foods is prohibited, but exemptions are granted under closely specified conditions. It is, perhaps, of interest to speculate what would have happened to other forms of preservation e.g. by heat, if all the effects and hazards could have been foreseen.

The commercial application of radiation has so far, been limited to a few restricted operations round the world e.g. inhibiting sprouting of potatoes in store and the disinfestation of grain; it is probable, however, that they will increase. Because of this and because most of the problems in the way of quick development are biological it is worth devoting some space to food irradiation.

Irradiation in this context means treatment with ionizing radiation and does not include infra-red or ultra-violet radiation. Ionizing radiation covers electromagnetic radiation of short wave-length (X-rays from machines and gamma radiation arising from the nuclear disintegration of radioactive substances), fast charged particles such as electrons, protons and alpha particles, and uncharged particles such as neutrons. Of all these types of radiation those most used in the irradiation of food are gamma radiation from radioactive sources such as cobalt 60 and, to a lesser extent, X-radiation and machine-produced fast electrons.

3.6.1   Possible applications of ionizing radiation

The use of ionizing radiations has been proposed and tried for many food treatments, not all of them preservation treatments as generally understood. (A list of these is given in Table 1, Ministry of Health, 1964). The unit of dose used in the table is the Mrad (Megarad) which is 1 rad $\times 10^6$. The rad is a unit based on the energy absorbed by the material irradiated, one rad is 100 erg $(10^{-5}$ J$)$ of energy released in one gram of irradiated matter from the applied radiation. The older unit, the Röntgen defines the amount of radiation applied, for foods or tissues approximately 1.07 Röntgen can result in the absorption of 1 rad.

The action of ionizing radiation in destroying micro-organisms and inhibiting the sprouting of root crops is not fully understood. Possibly it is due to the high sensitivity to such radiation of intracellular deoxyribo-nucleic acid and the related substance ribonucleic acid which together influence cellular reproduction and the synthesis of protein upon which reproduction depends. When a micro-organism dies after treatment with, e.g. 6 Mrad or less of radiation, death may not occur immediately after irradiation but at, or following the next reproductive division of the cell (Ministry of Health, 1964). Usually the cells injured by radiation can still reproduce by division, but once only, and if the resulting daughter cells are unable to reproduce they ultimately die. On the other hand should they be able to reproduce then a mutant strain of the cell will be produced since the genetic substance, deoxyribonucleic acid, of the parent cell has been altered by the radiation.

Mutations induced in this or any other manner are rarely viable or very distinctive. However, there is the danger that a non-pathogenic micro-organism may be transformed into a pathogen with high resistance to ionizing radiations and other treatments such as heat.

Table 1   Some possible applications of ionizing radiation in the treatment of food (Ministry of Health, 1964)

Purpose	Required action of the irradiation	Dose of irradiation needed (Mrad)
Sterilization of meat for subsequent storage at room temperature	Destruction of all micro-organisms and parasites including spores of *Cl. botulinum* if present	4–6
Sterilization of special ingredients of food, e.g. spices, celery seed	Destruction of bacteria liable to be present	1–3
An adjuvant to the use of heat for sterilization of food	Sensitization of bacterial spores to destruction by heat	0.5–1.0
Prevention of risk of salmonellae food-poisoning from, e.g. frozen egg, coconut, meat	Destruction of *salmonellae*	0.5–1.0
Extended cold storage 0 °C–4 °C) of carcase meat and pre-packed fish	Substantial reduction in numbers of spoilage bacteria mostly in vegetative form	0.3–0.5
Prolongation of storage life of fruit	Destruction of moulds	0.1–0.5
Disinfestation of stored grain	Destruction of insects	0.02
Elimination of any parasites in meats	Destruction of *Trichinella, Spiralis, Cysticercus bovis*	0.01
Prolongation of life of root crops, e.g. potatoes, onions	Inhibiting of sprouting	0.01
Hastening of ageing changes in alcoholic beverages	Chemical	1–2
Shortening of time needed for rehydration of dehydrated vegetables	Chemical or physical	0.25–2.5
Enhancement of odour of essential oils	Chemical	1

3.6.2   Pasteurization by irradiation

As already mentioned the heat treatment devised by Pasteur aimed at controlling spoilage organisms, but the term 'pasteurization' was later adopted for public health purposes to mean the destruction by heat in certain foods of pathogens such as *Mycobacterium tuberculosis*. Pasteurization by irradiation has been used to cover the control of organisms which cause food spoilage and also pathogens likely to be dangerous in the food which is to be irradiated. Examples of the use against spoilage organisms are the reduction of the number of organisms on meats and fish and of moulds on fruits such as strawberries; the doses required in these applications range from o.1 to 1 Mrad. An example of irradiation for pasteurization for the elimination of pathogens is the treatment of frozen whole egg against *Salmonellae*. An inactivation factor of 10^7 is achieved with a dose of 0.5 Mrad for the most radiation-resistant strain of *Salmonella* known.

3.6.3 Sterilization by irradiation

As in canning the objective in sterilizing by irradiation is the elimination of all organisms in the food without damaging its quality. In practice it may be defined as the reduction of the number of all contaminating organisms in a food to the point where none can be detected in the treated food by any recognised method, no matter how long the food is stored provided it is protected from recontamination.

Of all the micro-organisms likely to be present in food *Clostridium botulinum* in spore form is the least sensitive to destruction by irradiation (a possible exception to this is the non-pathogen *Micrococcus radiodurans*). This means that a dose less than 5 Mrad may destroy all the spoilage organisms present but leave viable spores of *Cl. botulinum*. If the subsequent storage conditions are suitable for the germination of the spores and proliferation of the vegetative organisms the production of *Cl. botulinum* toxin could occur without any of the warnings from the activities of other organisms. It is evident that care will be needed in the packaging and handling of foods given non-sterilizing doses.

3.6.4 Effects of irradiation on foods

The amount of energy released in a food even when a high dose is given is relatively small and the temperature change negligible. Consequently there is no 'cooking' effect, the food remains in its 'fresh' state.

However, the direct action of the radiation is mainly on the water molecules of the food, giving rise to intensely active H and OH free radicals. These can react with organic molecules present giving chemical changes which may be sufficient to affect taste and odour. The changes in the main food constituents are small and not sufficient to reduce significantly the digestibility and energy (calorific) value of the food as a whole.

Small changes have been observed in proteins and carbohydrates while in fats many different substances containing carbonyl groups may be formed. Destruction in varying amounts of vitamins may occur but, within the limits of any likely treatments, these are of the same order as result from cooking.

The production of carbonyls and of other potentially dangerous substances even though in minute amounts has led to exhaustive testing of irradiated foods for hazards to health. No danger to health has been shown even from foods given in high doses. Test animals, mice, rats, dogs and monkeys, have survived with little or no harm, many for several generations when fed such foods. There does not appear to be any hazard from induced radioactivity in the foods provided unduly high (above 5 MeV) radiation energies are not used.

3.6.5   Most likely applications

Although the advantages of 'cold sterilization' are attractive it is likely that the difficulties with 'off' flavours and odours at the relatively high doses needed for safety will divert attention more towards specialized uses and to pasteurization. The extension of the refrigerated storage life of poultry and fish for even a week or so could have a major effect on present marketing practices.

3.7   Other methods of preservation

There are many other methods of food preservation, many of them of considerable antiquity. They depend on controlling the environment of the foodstuff in such a way that spoilage and pathogenic organisms either cannot survive or, if any do, cannot multiply. A previous heat treatment for the food is sometimes required to de-activate enzymes and so prevent autolysis.

The availability of water for micro-organisms can be reduced by the use of salt or sugars while the acidity of the medium can be controlled by acetic, lactic or other acids. During the latter part of the nineteenth century antiseptics such as formalin, borates, salicylates and sulphites were freely used. Now they are either banned or strictly controlled.

3.7.1   Dry-salting

Dry-salting has long been used for the preservation of fish and meat and is still an important industry for fish in various parts of the world; 'salt cod' is highly favoured in, e.g. the West Indies where it is imported from Canada and Newfoundland. For the best results the fish is beheaded, split and gutted, then well cleaned. It is then placed in alternate layers, fish and salt, in barrels or water-tight containers and, as water is extracted from the fish, a brine is formed which eventually permeates the fish completely. The amount of salt required is about one-third that of the weight of the fish. This varies somewhat with the temperature and the size and kind of fish. It is important that good quality refined salt be used. After the salt has thoroughly penetrated it the fish may be packed in fresh brine or removed for drying either in the air and sun or artificially.

Spoilage occurs in salt-fish products because of chemical and biological changes. Some are due to autolysis caused by the enzymes in the tissues while others are due to bacteria which may be present in large numbers if the fish has not been well cleaned. This deterioration may be reduced by storage at low temperatures.

A problem encountered with the storage of salted cod and similar fish is the appearance of a reddish pigment on the surface of the flesh. This is caused by halophilic micro-organisms which are frequently found associated with solar salt, i.e. salt from the sea or salt-lakes evaporated in pans by heat from the sun and either not refined or inadequately refined.

Preservation of meat by dry-salting is a traditional method still practised in some parts of the world, e.g. Brazil, where pig meat in various cuts freed from visible fat is salted and packed in salt. Beef, also in Brazil, is salted in a more sophisticated way to give a product known as 'charque'. Cuts in the form of sheets of more or less uniform thickness are placed in vats of saturated brine and kept submerged by poling. A typical discoloration of the meat indicates when penetration of the brine is sufficient, about forty minutes. The sheets are drained and then salted by piling them in alternate layers of salt and meat. This is repeated several times and then the excess salt removed and the sheets dried in the sun on wooden racks. The sheets are then piled and covered to hold the heat from the sun and to allow them to settle. This drying and settling operation is repeated three or four times. This is an interesting process which has not been fully investigated technologically or biologically.

3.7.2 Pickling, curing and smoking

Modern methods of pickling and curing use salt, vinegar, lactic acid, sodium nitrate and nitrite. Such treatments combined with smoking are used in the production of bacon and hams from pork. The products, while lightly preserved, are produced now more to satisfy the consumers' tastes than for prolonged storage.

3.7.3 Chemical preservation

The use of considerable amounts of bacteriocides is no longer permitted. In fact it may be said that public, medical and scientific opinion is against the use of additives in general and preservatives in particular unless their use can be shown to be necessary and no harmful effects are to be expected. Their use today is closely controlled and emphasis is placed more on reducing or eradicating contamination of food by micro-organisms, through good hygiene in its preparation rather than relying on chemical agents for their destruction.

3.7.4 Preservatives

In the 'Preservatives in Food Regulations, 1962' a preservative is defined as 'any substance which is capable of inhibiting, retarding or arresting the process of fermentation, acidification or other deterioration of food or of masking any of the evidence of putrefaction'. This is a very wide definition which includes many substances which are added in traditional methods of preserving such as smoking and curing, herbs, spices, antioxidants and even the use of carbon-dioxide or nitrogen in the packing of food in hermetically sealed containers. Accordingly the regulations contain a long list of exceptions covering traditional methods and substances whose use is controlled by other regulations.

The list of permitted preservatives is quite short:

  (a) sulphur dioxide
  (b) propionic acid
  (c) sorbic acid
  (d) sodium nitrate
  (e) sodium nitrite
  (f) benzoic acid
  (g) methyl para-hydroxybenzoate
  (h) propyl para-hydroxybenzoate
  (i) tetracyclines
  (j) orthophenylphenol
  (k) copper carbonate.

Some are relatively widely used, e.g. sulphur dioxide while others have limited application, e.g. copper carbonate is limited to pears and then to not more than 5 parts per million (of copper) residue. Each use is closely defined in terms of the foodstuff and the maximum amount of preservative permitted in it. Thus for bread when propionic acid is used to control the development of 'rope' (*B. mesentericum*) its amount is limited to 3000 parts per million while sulphur dioxide in grape juice (unfermented, intended for sacramental use) must not exceed 70 parts per million.

3.7.5   Antibiotics

Antibiotics are substances which have an adverse effect on the growth of bacteria. They are produced naturally by living organisms, usually moulds, and can diffuse into their surroundings where they slow down or stop the growth of bacteria or kill them. Nowadays the naturally occurring antibiotics and modifications of them can be synthesized.

Some antibiotics, such as penicillin, are effective against a wide range of bacteria and are known as broad-spectrum antibiotics while others are effective against only a few types of bacteria.

The use of nisin in canning and for some processed cheeses and cheese spreads has already been mentioned. The use of the tetracyclines in ice for maintaining the freshness of fish has also been briefly noticed.

According to the Food and Drugs' Preservatives in Food Regulations (1962) (Statutory Instrument, 1962, No. 1532) cheese, clotted cream or any canned food may contain nisin as may any food prepared from one or other of the above.

In the U.K. the use of tetracyclines is limited to fish, application being made via the crushed ice in which the fish are packed in the holds of the fishing vessels. Alternative methods are: (i) dipping the fish, usually as fillets, in the antibiotic solution and then storing on ordinary ice or (ii)

Cʙ

stowing the whole fish in refrigerated sea water that contains the antibiotic in solution. The amount of tetracyclines permitted in fish under the Preservative in Food Regulations (1962) is 5 ppm.

In the U.S.A. eviscerated poultry are treated in cooling tanks of ice-water containing 10–20 ppm of a tetracycline for about two hours with subsequent storage at about 3 °C. A maximum of 7 ppm is permitted in raw poultry by the Food and Drugs Administration but this tolerance must not be exceeded in any part of the poultry. Usually the cooked bird contains no detectable residues though, very occasionally, levels up to 0.4 ppm have been found in the skin.

When tetracyclines are used on poultry in the U.S.A. the antibiotics are made available only to the packing stations which conform to certain standards of hygiene. This is said to be because tetracyclines are most effective when hygiene is good but there is the possibility that the use of such preservatives may mask poor hygiene control. So far the use of tetracyclines in the U.K. has been limited to ice for fish stowage.

It should perhaps be noted that the two tetracyclines in use are chlortetracycline and oxytetracycline either of which seems equally effective. Chlortetracycline is marketed for medical use in Britain under the trade name Aureomycin but is not used in its pure form for preserving fish. It is mixed with other chemicals which are harmless in food but which help to ensure that the antibiotics will be evenly distributed and active when in solution, particularly in tap water which may contain small quantities of substances which make the antibiotic inactive. The trade name of this preparation of Aureomycin is *Acronize*.

Oxytetracycline is marketed for medical use under the trade name Terramycin and when made up in a soluble form similar to chlortetracycline has the trade name *Biostat*.

The use of antibiotics is carefully regulated. There is a danger that use even in low concentrations may encourage the growth of resistant races of undesirable bacteria decreasing the value of the use of antibiotics against both pathogenic and food spoilage organisms.

3.7.6   Antioxidants

Antioxidants are dealt with separately in food legislation. There are many of these naturally present in foods so the statutory definition is framed to exclude most but to control closely the addition of specific substances to foods. The Antioxidant in Food Regulations (1966) defines antioxidants as follows: 'Antioxidant' means any substance which delays, retards or prevents the development in food of rancidity or other flavour deterioration due to oxidation but does not include lecithin, ascorbic acid, or its salts or esters, tocopherols, citric acid, tartaric acid, phosphoric acid or any permitted preservative, permitted emulsifier, permitted stabilizer or permitted colouring matter.

The permitted antioxidants are few in number:

   (a) propyl, octyl or dodecyl gallate
       or any mixture of them
   (b) butylated hydroxyanisole (BHA)
   (c) butylated hydroxytoluene (BHT)
   (d) and ethoxyquin (for apples and pears at the low limit of 3 parts per
       million)

The use is specified for edible oils and fats whether hardened or not and vitamin oils and concentrates, for partial glycerol esters, butter for manufacturing purposes and essential oils and isolates from the concentrates of essential oils.

The permitted limits of antioxidant range from 80 ppm for the gallates in butter for manufacturing purposes to 1000 ppm for gallates, BHA, BHT and any mixture of BHA and BHT in essential oils. A specific provision is made for preparations containing more than 100 000 IU's of vitamin A per gramme where 10 ppm is permitted for each 1000 IU's per gramme.

4 Food Manufacturing

Food manufacturing industries are varied and account for a large proportion of the food consumed. They complement the industries engaged in food preservation and may be considered in many instances to be extensions of the process of preservation. They include milling and baking, meat processing, fish processing, the production of edible oils and fats, sugar refining, fruit processing, the manufacture of cocoa, chocolate and sugar confectionery and the fermentation industries yielding beer, wines and spirits.

It is not possible to give comprehensive descriptions of each industry in a booklet of this size, accordingly a selection has been made illustrative, it is hoped, of some of the major manufacturing industries.

4.1 Milling and baking industries

These industries, having as their end product a wide variety of baked goods, form probably the largest single section of the food manufacturing industry in the United Kingdom. All cereal-based foods taken together contribute nearly 30% of the energy (calorific) value of the diet. Bread and flour alone contribute approximately 18% which indicates the reliance placed on cereal products for a staple contribution to the diet. The total annual expenditure on the products of the baking industry was some £729 m. in 1969, or about a quarter of the total expenditure on processed food.

MILLING. The milling industry in the U.K. is mainly concerned with the milling of wheat the total usage of which is about 5 m. tonnes per year of which about 1.7 m. tonnes is home-grown and the remainder imported. This 5 m. tonnes is converted into 3.6 m. tonnes of flour for human consumption and 1.4 m. tonnes of wheatfeed for animal consumption. The consumption of flour per head of the population in Britain has fallen since 1953 but the decrease has been approximately balanced by increased population and a decline in imports. Thus total flour production has remained more or less unchanged over the past few years.

4.1.1 The wheat grain

The wheat grain is the fruit (caryopsis) of the wheat plant, a cultivated grass. It consists mainly of reserve compounds, carbohydrates, nitrogenous substances (mainly proteins), fats, mineral salts and water together with small quantities of other substances such as vitamins. The carbohydrates, which are the major constituents, form about 82% of the dry matter of the grain; they include starch (the largest constituent), cellulose, pentosans, dextrins and sugars. The digestible carbohydrates are important nutrients but the crude fibre is indigestible and of little positive nutritional importance. Most wheats contain about 8–16% of protein and small amounts (2–4%) of liquids.

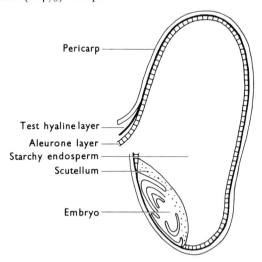

Pericarp

Test hyaline layer
Aleurone layer
Starchy endosperm
Scutellum

Embryo

Fig. 4-1   Diagram of section of cereal grain

Figure 4-1 illustrates the structure of the wheat grain in section. The outer layers which include the pericarp, seed coat and aleurone layers are called *bran* for milling purposes. The inner portion of the grain consisting of about four-fifths of its total weight is called the *endosperm* and consists essentially of starch granules embedded in a continuous matrix of protein. The *germ* prominent at one end of the grain consists of the embryo and the scutellum (cotyledon). Table 2 shows the distribution of the wheat constituents in the main morphological parts of the grain.

4.1.2   The milling process

About 84% of all bread sold in the United Kingdom is white, 9% is brown including wholemeal and wheatmeal, and 7% consists of speciality types. The millers aim normally is to produce mainly white flour and for this purpose the endosperm only is required in the milled product. The bran is rejected because of the undesired colour which it gives the flour and also because it contributes indigestible fibre. The germ is rejected because of its high oil content which reduces the storage life of the flour due to the development of rancidity and also because it contains sulphur compounds which have a deleterious effect on loaf volume.

The main objectives of the milling process are (a) to separate pure endosperm from bran and germ to give flour of suitable granularity, free from bran specks and of good colour and storage life, and (b) to obtain the maximum amount of endosperm as flour thus attaining the maximum extraction rate (the percentage of wheat converted to flour) consistent with the above requirements.

Separated germ is used in speciality foods; and the bran plus some germ and residual adhering endosperm is obtained as wheatfeed, used primarily in animal feeding.

In order to achieve the required separation the modern milling process involves a form of grinding which is a combination of shearing, scraping and crushing which exploits the differences in physical properties between the endosperm, bran and germ. Present day milling is based on the steel roller-milling developed in Hungary, where the first complete roller-mill was operated in 1860. The new process had been widely adopted in the United Kingdom by the end of the nineteenth century.

Table 2

Part	Wt (g per 100 g of grain)	Constitutents (% of total)				
		Starch	Protein	Fibre	Fat	Ash
Pericarp, seedcoat, aleurone	15	0	20	93	30	67
Endosperm	82	100	72	4	50	23
Embryo, scutellum	3	0	8	3	20	10

The wheat is first cleaned to remove impurities and conditioned to optimum moisture content. It is then ground in a succession of 15–20 grinding stages with interspersed sifting stages and purification (by air separation) of the intermediate products. There are two types of mill roll surface, fluted or corrugated rolls used on the 'break' mills and smooth rolls used on the 'reduction' mills. The break rolls open the whole grain and scrape endosperm from the bran while the reduction rolls reduce coarse particles of endosperm to flour. There is a speed differential between each pair of rolls, greater in the case of the break rolls than the reduction rolls, so that the former have a shearing action while the latter have a crushing action. Sieving is carried out with nests of sieves, called plansifters. This milling process is highly mechanised and uses little labour. Output per operative is about 1.6 times the average for all manufacturing industry.

Since the last war many technical changes have occurred in the milling industry. Productivity has increased as the number of units of production has decreased. Transport of flour and other particulate substances within the milling system is now carried out pneumatically rather than mechanically. *Air classification* techniques, which separate flour particles according to size, have made it possible to produce two or more flours of different protein content from the same parent flour, since there is a relationship between the size of endosperm fragments and their protein content.

4.1.3 Wheat quality

Wheat quality depends on (i) the behaviour of the grain in the mill (ii) the baking characteristics of the flour produced.

'Hardness' is a hereditary characteristic of wheats and is demonstrated by the way the endosperm breaks down during milling. Hard wheats yield coarse, gritty flour which is free flowing and easily sifted. Soft wheats yield finer flours which are not free flowing. Hard wheats are therefore easier for the miller to work than soft wheats. Hard wheats come mainly from Canada, the U.S.A., the U.S.S.R. and parts of Australia while most of the wheats grown in western European countries, including the United Kingdom, are soft.

The 'strength' of a wheat is shown by its ability to give flour which can be made into bread of good volume, crumb texture and keeping qualities. Strength in wheats is a varietal characteristic and high strength is usually associated with a high protein content. Large amounts of strong wheats are grown in Canada, the U.S.A., the U.S.S.R. and elsewhere, while most western European wheats including those grown in the United Kingdom are weak.

Hardness and strength are not closely linked genetically and appear to segregate separately. Nevertheless, in general, the countries growing strong wheats are also those that produce hard wheats. In general it may be said that the broad plains and climates of North America and the U.S.S.R. with their cold winters and hot summers favour the hard and strong varieties. Although relatively hard and strong varieties may be grown in Europe their yields are lower on the whole than soft and weak varieties. The British miller has to use his knowledge to choose and blend wheats to form a grist that will produce flour having the desired characteristics for particular purposes. Breadmaking grists in the U.K. normally contain substantial amounts (over 50%) of imported strong wheats, usually from Canada.

Wheat breeders in the U.K. as in other countries are continually trying to develop new improved wheat varieties.

The first aim is a reliable wheat of good yield and high resistance to disease, the second is to produce a grain more technically useful than its predecessors in terms of hardness and strength. The breeder normally hopes to attain both these objectives but may settle for one or the other depending on circumstances. The yields and disease resistance of English wheats have improved significantly in recent years but most of those grown today are still soft in character and at best of only medium strength. There is not sufficient home-grown wheat of good milling and breadmaking qualities to permit of very high proportions of home-grown wheat to be used in breadmaking grists. However, the situation has changed considerably since 1939 when a bread grist might contain little or no English wheat. It may now contain 25% or more when the harvest conditions permit, and the proportion is increasing. This is due both to the breeding of improved wheat varieties and to new breadmaking processes which permit the use of increased proportions of weak wheats in the grist.

The soft English wheats may not be ideal for breadmaking flours but they do produce excellent flours for biscuit and cake manufacture where high protein contents are not necessary and may even be undesirable. About 90% of the wheat used for cake and biscuit flours is home-grown while about 50% of the wheat used in the manufacture of household flour (plain or self-raising) is home-grown.

4.1.4 Baking

The industry produces a large variety of breads, cakes and biscuits. Bread is the largest component of the baking industry, 72% of all the flour produced in the U.K. goes into its manufacture. Cake and biscuit production uses about 14% of total U.K. flour output.

In recent years there have been important changes both in the structure and the technology of the baking. Production units have become larger and their numbers reduced. Increasing mechanization of the production process has occurred for all types of baked goods.

4.1.5 Breadmaking

The conventional break-making process, which, until fairly recently, was responsible for virtually all the bread produced in the U.K. has persisted largely unchanged for hundreds of years. It consists of mixing flour, yeast, salt and water together to produce a dough which is then allowed to ferment for about three hours. This is called bulk fermentation and various biochemical changes occur during this period, the chief of which are (1) the production of carbon dioxide by the yeast fermenting the sugars naturally present in the flour together with those produced by the action of amylase on wheat starch and (2) the changes which take place in the protein structure making the dough more elastic and capable of retaining the gas produced during the fermentation and baking.

After bulk fermentation, the dough is divided into pieces of suitable weight, which are allowed to rest for a few minutes. They are then moulded into the final shape and placed in tins, allowed to rise for about 45 minutes and baked, usually at a temperature of 232 °C for 30 minutes. Variations of this basic process and of the starting ingredients enable a great variety of white, brown and speciality breads to be made but the most popular form today is the white, sliced and wrapped loaf.

Attempts have been made, particularly during the past 25 years, to speed up the basic process and make it more amenable to mechanisation. In the middle 1950s continuous breadmaking processes developed in the U.S.A. were introduced into the U.K. These were not found to be commercially viable and the first really successful development came with the introduction of the Chorleywood Bread Process in 1961. This process eliminates the three-hour bulk fermentation stage by using the mixing stage to replace it with a controlled amount of very intense mechanical working, lasting only a few minutes, which greatly simplifies control of the dough-making stage. This working changes the elastic properties of the dough proteins mechanically instead of biochemically, and saves much time. The process requires the use of an oxidative 'improver' (e.g. ascorbic acid) and fat in the dough and also a higher level of yeast than is used in the conventional process. In addition to savings in time and space there are advantages in that the yield of bread from flour is increased due to reduction in fermentation losses and flours of lower protein may be used. The bread produced is of excellent quality and is said to be superior to conventional bread in volume, texture and staling properties (see Fig. 4–2).

Fig. 4–2 Fully automatic one-sack Tweedy mixer for bread dough. The mixing chamber can be seen at the bottom of the picture. The control panel is on the right. (Photograph by courtesy of the Flour Milling and Baking Research Association)

Processes of this type, known as mechanical development processes, have aroused much interest outside the U.K. and have been successfully modified into continuous bread-making systems.

Other developments include the activated dough process in which a mixture of oxidising and reducing agents is used to produce the desired properties in the dough in place of the intense mechanical work employed in the Chorleywood Bread Process. This process has the advantage of eliminating the necessity for the baker to buy special high speed mixing equipment. It cannot yet be used commercially in the U.K. as the reducing agent required is not, under the present regulations, a permitted additive to bread.

4.1.6 Biscuit and cake manufacture

In the making of biscuits a dough is first made by mixing together flour, water, fat, sugar and other ingredients. Several different processes may be used in forming the mixed dough into a biscuit shaped dough piece according to the type of biscuit required. In one common method the dough is forced into a continuous sheet by passing through rollers and from this sheet dough pieces are stamped out. The dough pieces are then baked at a suitable temperature for the appropriate time (see Fig. 4–3) and then wrapped in packets of fixed weight. The process is one which has been highly mechanized for a long time and most recent developments have been concerned with improving control of the different stages of the process,

Fig. 4–3 A modern biscuit oven. (Photograph by courtesy of McVitie and Price, and Simon-Vicars Ltd.)

and where possible, rendering such control automatic. There are systems available to the biscuit manufacturer for automatic control of dough-mixing and of the thickness of the dough sheet.

The biscuit manufacturer has been able to make good use of the development of bulk-handling systems for ingredients and such systems now handle flour, fat and sugar in bulk form. Control systems have been developed with the bulk handling so that different recipes can be selected by push-button.

The one stage of biscuit manufacture which is not continuous is the mixing. There have been various attempts to achieve satisfactory continuous mixing of biscuit doughs but none of them has been adopted to any significant extent.

The production of cakes is the baking operation least susceptible to mechanization and process control. This is due to the very large variety of cakes made and to the complexity of the operations involved. However, there have been, in recent years, some developments in the continuous production of certain types of cake, especially Swiss Roll. The most recent development in this field has been the introduction of continuous mixing of cake batters, which combined with automatic depositing and the use of travelling ovens has made the production of this type of cake a continuous process (Fig. 4–4).

Fig. 4–4 Modern continuous mixing equipment for cake production. (Photograph by courtesy of E. T. Oakes Ltd.)

4.2 Margarine

Margarine has a relatively short history, a mere one hundred years or so. The original patent was taken out in 1869 in England by Mège Mouriès, but the products now included as margarine bear little resemblance to his pressed beef suet.

Beef suet pressed at 30°–40 °C yielded a fat melting at 20°–25 °C which had, relative to butter, a poor texture and an insipid flavour. However, it sold and was, apparently, used considerably as a diluent for butter. This adulteration led to the Margarine Act of 1887 which defined butter and margarine and made their mixing illegal. Later legislation has recognized the nutritional and 'quality' values of modern margarines and their place in modern diets. Now it is a matter of controlling the addition of butter to margarine which must be declared, the water content must not exceed 16% and vitamins A and D must be added (27–33 IU per g of vitamin A and 2.8–3.5 IU per g of vitamin D).

4.2.1 Raw materials

Present day margarine is prepared from blends of vegetable and animal oils and fats with which cultured or sweet fat-free or whole milk is added to form an emulsion of water in fat. The culturing of the pasteurized milk is done with the lactic acid forming *B. acidilactis* and the flavour producing *Streptococcus cremoris* and *S. diacetylactis* (these yield acetylmethylcarbinol and, especially, diacetyl).

The fats and oils used come from a wide range of sources, almost all of which are imported into the U.K. They include: palm oil (*Elaeis guincensis*), groundnut (*Arachis hypogaea*), coconut (*Cocos nucifera*), sunflower (*Helianthus annuus*), cottonseed (*Gossypium spp.*), soya bean (*Glycine soja*), beef and mutton tallow, herring and pilchard oils; whale oil has also been largely used in the past but supplies have now dwindled.

Fats and oils are triglycerides, esters of glycerol and fatty acids. Those with lower melting points than normal room temperature are oils, those with higher melting points are fats. One molecule of glycerol combines, with the elimination of water, with three molecules of fatty acid which may be saturated or unsaturated. In saturated fatty acids all the carbon atoms except the end carboxyl group have their full complement of hydrogen atoms, e.g. stearic acid: $CH_3(CH_2)_{16}COOH$ while in unsaturated fatty acids double bonds occur between some carbon atoms e.g. $CH_3(CH_2)_4CH{:}CHCH_2CH{:}CH(CH_2)_7COOH$ linoleic acid. Some unsaturated fatty acids are 'essential' in the nutritional sense, in that they are necessary to the body which cannot of itself synthesize them. They are generally referred to as polyunsaturated acids and the most important is linoleic acid. Linolenic and arachidonic acids can be formed in the body from linoleic acid. It is believed by many nutritionists and others that an adequate supply of essential fatty acids in the diet reduces the risk of heart failure; it reduces the cholesterol level in the bloodstream.

There is a wide range of fatty acids in fats and oils and in each glyceride; the three acid components are rarely the same. The main acids are:

Saturated
Lauric	$CH_3(CH_2)_{10}COOH$
Myristic	$CH_3(CH_2)_{12}COOH$
Palmitic	$CH_3(CH_2)_{14}COOH$

Unsaturated
Oleic	$CH_3(CH_2)_7CH:CH(CH_2)_7COOH$
Palmitoleic	$CH_3(CH_2)_5CH:CH(CH_2)_7COOH$
Linoleic	$CH_3(CH_2)_4CH:CH\ CH_2CH:CH(CH_2)_7COOH$

4.2.2 *Manufacture*

The first stage in the manufacture of modern margarines is the refining of the raw oils and fats, i.e. making them free of taste, odour and colour. The fat-insoluble impurities are removed by 'degumming'. The crude oil is mixed with water or a weak salt solution into which gums, resins, proteins and phosphatides separate. This watery layer is then run off. The oil is then neutralized which turns the free fatty acids into soaps which are separated from the oil. The separated oil is washed and dried *in vacuo*. Neutralization with sodium hydroxide has a slight bleaching effect on the oil but the major bleaching is by addition of Fuller's earth to the oil while still under vacuum. This absorbs colouring materials and materials which would affect stability. The oil is pumped to filter presses where the Fuller's earth is removed.

It is at this stage that hydrogenation is done. This can be controlled so that the level of saturation of the oil can be that desired in the product. The process is the addition of hydrogen atoms to the double bonds in the fat or oil molecules in the presence of the catalyst, highly refined powdered nickel. The nickel is removed by filtration after the reaction.

Hydrogenation has made it possible to use previously difficult oils such as fish oils to supplement and replace vegetable and whale oils and fats.

Esterification is another method of modifying the melting points of fats, this time by changing the positions of the fatty acid groups in the glyceride molecules. The fat is heated in the presence of a catalyst (sodium, sodium ethoxide or sodium methoxide) to a temperature of 110°–160 °C and the fatty acid groups rearrange themselves in a random manner which may be intramolecular or intermolecular.

After these treatments the oil is again bleached and filtered and finally heated to 160°–180 °C and steam distilled *in vacuo* (2–8 mm). The steam distillation removes the odiferous materials produced during the processing.

The oils are blended to give the melting point, plasticity and consistency to suit the climate and use for which the margarine is intended.

Additives other than the legally required vitamins are salt, colouring materials, emulsifiers and flavouring agents. Salt acts partly as a preservative and partly as a flavour inducing agent. The most commonly used colouring material in Great Britain is annatto, a yellow orange dye from the seeds of the roucou tree (*Bixa orellana*). Beta-carotene is also used. The main emulsifiers used are monoglycerides and lecithin, flavouring materials are constituents of butter, e.g. butyric acid, caproic acid and delta-lactones.

The final stages are emulsification, chilling and texturing. In the modern processes these take place in a 'Votator' cylinder. In this the material undergoes vigorous stirring, cooling, crystallization and kneading. Usually there is a post-crystallization tube where the cooled emulsion completes its crystallization and which is connected directly to the packaging machine. In this process the product moves in a closed machine safe from atmospheric contamination, is untouched by hand and is therefore hygienic. This stage, including packing, lasts only 1–2 minutes.

4.3 Cooking fats

Blends of oils and fats chilled and texturized in the same way as margarine are used for shortening the structure of dough, for cake-making, for filling creams and for frying. They need a soft texture, good creaming properties, freedom from foaming in frying and should not become rancid.

These requirements limit, to some extent, the selection of raw materials, coconut and palm kernel oils cannot be used because they are liable to cause foaming when mixed with other oils. Creamability is increased by whipping in at least 10 per cent of an inert gas before chilling the fat.

4.4 Cooking oils

These are used for frying and in salad dressings. They consist of one or a blend of unsaturated oils. The commonest are olive, groundnut, sunflower, soya bean and maize.

4.5 Other manufactured products

It is not possible in the small compass of this booklet to describe others of the many manufactured food and drink products. It is suggested that specialized publications of which examples are given in 'Recommended further reading' at the end of this work should be consulted.

The subjects suggested for study are:

    (a) meat products
    (b) fish products
    (c) fruit products
    (d) sugar
    (e) cocoa, chocolate and sugar confectionery
    (f) beer, wines and spirits

The subject of food manufacture cannot be left without illustrating the extent of control in a modern factory (Fig. 4–5) over the materials used in its various products.

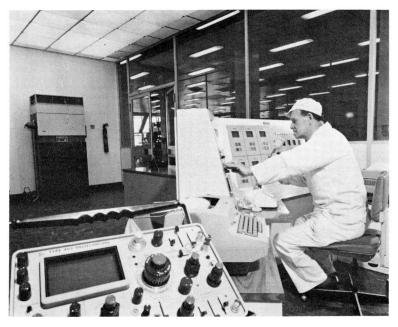

Fig. 4–5 Computer room for the Materials Handling System of a food factory. The operator is using the intercom system which links all sections of the plant. The oscilloscope (bottom left) is used for checking the computer. At the end of the room is an air cooling unit. Beyond the glass screen is part of the main manufacturing area. (Photograph by courtesy of H. J. Heinz Co. Ltd.)

5 New Foods

5.1 Convenience foods

Much of the food we eat today would have seemed novel to our recent ancestors. From earliest times efforts have been made to make food more convenient from the point of view of storing, distributing, preparing and cooking. But in the past quarter of a century the emergence of foods in a greater state of preparedness for the table has led to the words 'convenience foods' having a special connotation. They are not 'new foods' in the sense now becoming generally accepted but they deserve some consideration here before the various relatively new forms of food which technology is bringing into being.

In the reports of the National Food Survey Committee convenience foods are defined as "those processed foods for which the degree of preparation has been carried to an advanced stage by the manufacturer and which may be used as labour-saving alternatives to less highly processed products. The convenience foods distinguished by the Survey are cooked and canned meats, meat products, cooked and canned fish, fish products, canned vegetables, vegetable products, canned fruit, fruit juices, cakes and pastries, biscuits, breakfast cereals, puddings (including canned milk puddings), cereal products, instant coffee and coffee essences, baby foods, canned soups, dehydrated soups, ice-cream bought to serve with a meal, and all 'cabinet trade' quick frozen foods but not uncooked poultry or uncooked whitefish."

This definition is very wide and shows the extent to which convenience foods had come to be taken for granted before the term was even used for them. One tends to think of such foods being 'frozen whole meals' as sold in retail shops or as used both in restaurant and hospital catering but in fact the number of defined convenience foods on the market is very large. Convenience foods, including those used in catering, now hold some 25% of the total food market and it is likely that more and more will be used as housewives increasingly work outside the home.

There is likely to be increasing development of 'heat-in', 'serve-in' packages and advances in polymer chemistry will allow extensive use of plastics resistant to high temperature. Already flexible pouches have been used for thermal processing in an attempt to provide an alternative to the conventional tin can. It is probable that further progress in food technology will increase the number of flexible packages used both for processing in the factory and for 'boil-in-the-bag' preparation at home. It is evident that the housewife is increasingly ready to accept 'convenience' foods which have good storage properties and are lighter in weight than canned foods.

Development in the packaging of these foods is taking place all the time and is an essential part of their present and future success. In particular the rapid expansion of vending machine marketing of foods creates a demand for new types of container easy to open and from which the contents may be readily eaten.

5.2 Vegetable 'meats'

Simulated meats have been developed to varying levels of acceptability from oilseed proteins; soya, sunflower, cottonseed and groundnuts. The stimulus for this effort arises from the shortage, on a world-wide basis, of animal protein and also the expensive and inefficient nature of animal conversion of vegetable materials into protein. As much of 90% of the protein fed to many animals is used by the animal to maintain itself and frequently only 10–15% is recovered as animal products suitable for use by man as food. The production of beefsteak from alfalfa or soybean meal is about 7% efficient; if the soybean meal could be consumed directly by man the equivalent efficiency would be about 70%. However, soybean meal (containing about 50% protein) is not attractive as a food for man because it contains a high proportion of indigestible components of the cell structure of the bean. Its use has been mainly as cattle food.

Efforts have been made to use oilseed proteins in the form of simulated meat and meat products and a fair amount of success is being attained. The proteins from the oilseed residues have been purified and can be spun into very fine fibrils.

The proteins from de-fatted seeds are extracted with mild alkali and refined to give a bland isolate of 95–98% purity. The isolate as an alkaline dispersion is extruded through spinnerettes into a coagulating bath where the formation of fibres occurs. The fibres, the properties of which can be varied during treatment to produce tender, delicate fibrils or tough strands, are then drawn away by pick up rolls each 'tow' of monofilaments consisting of 16 000 individual members. The diameter of the fibres can be varied as required.

The fibres after washing and various treatments can be spun or knitted into 'textured' products. The treatments usually consist of the addition of fat, colour flavourings, supplemental nutrients, protein binders (e.g. egg albumen) and stabilizers followed by processing in a blender-cooker. The products are analogous to cooked meat and, with some exceptions, can be used in the same way, i.e. they can be eaten direct or they can be frozen, canned or dehydrated.

D B

In spun products* the texture producing fibrils seldom constitute more than 40% of the dry weight; the remainder consists of the fat, flavours, protein binder etc. added during treatment in the blender-cooker. A typical composition (on a dry basis) is 40% fibres, 30% flavours, colours and added nutrients, 20% fat and 10% protein binding system. In a ready-to-eat state most of these products contain 50–70% of water. They may provide more protein and less fat than meats as their composition and hence nutritive value can be closely controlled. Unlike meat these products also contain carbohydrates which are introduced with the flavours, colours and nutrients. Protein, fat, vitamin and mineral content can be adjusted to suit special dietary requirements or preferences, e.g. for low energy (calorie) items of food.

Soya protein is relatively low in sulphur amino acids but this nutritional disadvantage can be overcome by appropriate supplementation with amino acids or suitable proteins. The anti-nutritional factors present in soybeans are destroyed during processing.

These meat flavoured vegetable proteins can either be used to dilute the meat component of some foods such as hamburgers or they can be used to replace meat or fish completely. It is possible to simulate the texture, flavour and other characteristics of ham, fish and fish products, chicken and roast beef and several commercial organizations in the U.S.A. are engaged in developing such foods.

Meat analogues can be derived from defatted soya flour without 'spinning' which reduces their cost. The process involves increasing the water content of the flour, raising the temperature and extruding the mass through a predetermined die size at a controlled temperature (about 121 °C). This extrusion process gives the protein 'direction' and the texture is 'set'. It can be flavoured, before extrusion to resemble chicken, ham or bacon and can be available as chunks, granules, dice or strips.

A typical texturized vegetable protein (TVP) made by this method contains 50% protein, 1% fat, 3% fibre, 8% moisture, 6% ash and 32% carbohydrate. It is a porous, dry material which when slightly hydrated will absorb oils; when fully hydrated by cooking in water for 10–25 minutes and absorbing 2–3 times its weight of water, it becomes tender and chewable. All essential amino acids are present but the sulphur ones, methionine and cystine, are limiting; however when TVP is used in conjunction with meat the amino acid balance is generally restored by the amino acid contribution from the meat.

These products at the present stage of development are not cheap and legally cannot be sold as meat. However, costs should come down when production increases and there are evident advantages when comparison is made with uncooked carcase meat. Spun protein products are cooked

---

* An example of a spun vegetable protein food now marketed in the U.S.A. is 'Bontrue' produced by General Mills Inc. Another example expected to be marketed in the U.K. before this book is published is 'Kesp' developed by Courtaulds from the field bean (*The Times*, 12th September 1972).

during manufacture which has to be taken into account when comparing costs with uncooked carcase meat. The hand trimming inspection and supervision stages necessary in a conventional meat processing plant are eliminated in meat analogue manufacture.

So far textured vegetable protein is marketed in Britain in a limited way but there appears no reason why its use should not increase both in the home and for catering. Under present legislation it will be necessary for products of this nature to be sold in Britain under fully explanatory descriptions and not as meat diluents.

5.3 Leaf protein

The extraction of protein from leafy crops is economically perhaps the most attractive method of attacking the protein deficiency in much of the world population's diet. This is particularly so as yields are highest in areas (wet tropics) where the need is greatest.

The process which has been developed by Pirie at Rothamsted is relatively straightforward and based on methods long in use in the laboratory. Yields are good, even in Britain 1.4 tons per hectare of extracted protein have been obtained while in Mysore 3 tons have been reached (1 ton = 1.0161 tonne). (About 370 kg of protein would be available in bread produced from the yield of one hectare of wheat in the U.K.) The species of leafy plant does not appear to be important and by-products such as the leaves of peas, beans, early potatoes and sugar beet may be used; leaves of jute, ramie and sweet potato may be used in the tropics. Because the protein is washed, both neutral and acid, leaves that are toxic in the raw state can be used.

The crop is pulped at its own pH (usually 5.8–6.3) and water added during pulping to increase the water content of the pulp to 90–92%. The protein can be precipitated by adding salt or acid to the pressed juice but in large-scale work heat is used (> 70 °C) as this enables easy filtration of the curd. The curd is washed at about pH 4 to remove flavour and any alkaloids present and to give easy filtration. The product in this moist state has the keeping quality of cheese or sauerkraut. The press-cake is dark green and contains 40% dry matter of which 60–70% is protein. When possible it is used in this form but it can with care be dried, canned or preserved by pickling.

In its dark green form it is acceptable in West Africa, south-west India and in New Guinea. These regions are predominantly vegetarian or their inhabitants are accustomed to using dried leaves in powder form. Other forms of presentation have been made and have been or will be tried in places of greatest need. The main difficulty in the acceptance of leaf protein is, perhaps, its colour.

5.4 Single cell protein

The production of protein from yeasts for animal feeding has a history dating back at least to the 1914–18 war. Food yeasts, i.e. for human use, came into some prominence during World War II and much work is now being done on both development and production of protein from a variety of micro-organisms; fungi (including yeasts), bacteria and algae.

5.4.1 Fungi—yeasts

Yeasts have long been produced in bulk for brewing and for baking. There is, therefore, ample long standing experience of production. *Candida* (*Torula*) *utilis* has become the classical food yeast grown on carbohydrate substrates. *C. lipolytica* grows on hydrocarbon substrates. *Candida utilis* has the merit of fermenting pentoses as well as hexoses. It was reported (BUNKER, H. J., 1966) that in 1966 some quarter of a million tonnes of food yeast were being produced in different parts of the world and Russia planned an annual production of 900 000 tonnes by 1970 of food and fodder yeast.

It is evident that so far food yeast is making only a small contribution to the world's protein shortage. But in the world's continuing and increasing state of food shortage, particularly of protein, microbial sources can become increasingly valuable for both proteins and vitamins. The potential possibilities of single cell protein production compared with that of conventional meat are seen in the much quoted differences in yield between yeast and bullock:

bullock weighing 10 cwt. (508 kg) yields 1 lb (0.45 kg) protein/day (BUNKER, 1966)
yeast, 10 cwt. (508 kg) yields 50 tons (50.80 tonne) protein/day

This difference appears astonishing but is not so when it is appreciated that a freely growing single yeast under optimum conditions divides at approximately 20-minute intervals each cell then speedily growing to the size and weight of the parent cell. It is not surprising that increasing effort is being made in the development of such methods of increasing world protein supplies.

5.4.2 Bacteria

The number of bacterial species which have been grown for food is limited but increasing attention is now being given them since some have been found capable of using hydrocarbon substrates. Species of *Pseudomonas* and of methane oxidizers are now being used in the petroleum industry.

Other bacteria which have been mentioned as potential protein suppliers are:

Escherichia coli; has been used in cattle food but is not entirely acceptable.

Mycobacterium tuberculosis; this is stated to contain up to ten times as much methionine as yeast. But a pathogen can hardly be regarded as a likely candidate for cultivation.

Lactobacillus fermentans, *Alcaligenes viscosus* and *Escherichia coli* all contain more than 80% protein on a dry weight basis ($N \times 6.25$) so could merit closer examination as potential sources of protein if their amino acid patterns are favourable.

5.4.3   Algae

One of the staple human foods in the Sahara near Lake Chad is a rich soup prepared from 'cakes' known as dihé. These cakes are fibrous masses of the blue-green alga *Spirulina maxima*. These rather large algae cling together because of their spiral shape and so can be cheaply harvested by a rotary string filter instead of centrifuging. Their flavour is described as inoffensive and their protein content and amino acid pattern relatively favourable. They have not so far been reported as used for further than local commercial development.

The largest experimental unit for growing algae is in Czechoslovakia, a developed country but one short of protein for animal feed.

The organism grown is the green alga, *Scenedesmus quadricaula* which grows in four-cell units and is more readily managed and filtered than *Chlorella*. The pilot plant has had problems with infections by bacteria and protozoa but they appear to have been overcome. The largest unit is stated to be 900 square metres in area and to yield about 12 kg dry weight per day.

Although theoretically the algae should be the most attractive candidates for the production of 'single cell protein' because of their photosynthetic ability, in practice they have, so far, not been economic. They depend on climate, nature of substrate including a nitrogen supply and light availability.

5.5   Protein from oil

Some yeasts and bacteria produce protein from fractions of petroleum. The requirements for cell growth in a fermentation process are supplies of suitable sources of carbon, hydrogen, oxygen, nitrogen and of minerals. With some yeasts hydrocarbons can supply the carbon; only n-paraffins are readily assimilable but there are considerable differences in the acceptability of n-paraffins of different carbon numbers. Many organisms (particularly bacteria) will assimilate methane while n-paraffins in the range C_{12}–C_{20} (kerosenes) and upwards (gas oil) are readily assimilated by some yeasts. For some reason not yet known n–paraffins in the range C_2–C_{10} are not readily acceptable by either bacteria or yeasts.

The conditions for the fermentation require careful control or hydrocarbon consumption and heat production become excessive.

With normal paraffins as the carbon source about 50% of the carbon is incorporated in the biomass giving approximately an equal weight of cell production to that of the paraffin consumed. Rapid mass transfer of the oxygen from the gas phase (air) to the liquid phase is important as it is in this phase that assimilation takes place. Nitrogen is added as ammonia which also serves as a pH control. The minerals required are the same as for plant growth: P, K, Zn, etc., and are added as salts.

In the production processes all the components are brought together in continuous fermentation. There are three main process variants:

1. Where natural gas is the carbon source the gases can be fed in together and since there is little contamination from the methane the harvesting of the cells is relatively easy.
2. Where the substrate is crude oil, the oil is first refined into fractions and the selected fractions of n–paraffins separated and fermented. Since virtually all the paraffin is consumed the harvesting is relatively easy.
3. The total gas oil fraction can be fermented. However only about 10% of the oil is assimilated and the harvesting of the cells is more difficult as the hydrocarbons have to be separated by extraction.

Of these the last two only are in production or nearly so.

The product contains 60–70% of protein so is comparable with the soya and fish meal protein concentrates used for animal feeding. There have been no problems reported in persuading animals to accept 'oil protein' in their feed but more work on improving palatability is likely to be necessary before it can be used as human food.

On the safety side trials have been made over several years and through several generations of animals with no untoward effects. It is understood that it is possible to reduce levels of residual hydrocarbons to limits acceptable as safe.

5.5.1   Future of protein from oil

Although there is increasing effort on a world wide basis to develop this attractive new source of protein progress so far has been relatively small. However the need is there and the prospects appear good in the long run.

The Soviet Union is reported as producing at least 10 000 tonnes a year for cattle feed from crude oil products and aiming at a million tonnes a year. Czechoslovakia has a pilot plant fermenting unwanted fractions of crude oil and plans one of 100 000 tonnes capacity.

British Petroleum has a pilot plant producing 225 tonnes annually and plans to increase this considerably, Esso has a joint project with Nestlé on the production of protein for human consumption using a purified paraffin substrate while Shell in Great Britain have announced that they are working on a process using methane as the carbon substrate.

5.6 Problems of single cell protein

Although considerable advances have been made in production of single cell proteins and in assessing the nutritional values of the products problems still remain. There is a tendency towards bitterness in proteins from yeast. The relatively high concentration of nucleic acids in protein from yeasts and bacteria introduces both flavour and nutritional questions while if cell wall polysaccharides are included in the products problems of digestibility are introduced.

6 Quality and Nutritional Value

It is evident that although the nutritional value of a food is in the food its effects can only be observed if the food is eaten. Hence there is not only a natural desire that a food should look and taste good but if nutritional requirements are to be satisfied there is also a necessity that it should be sufficiently attractive to be eaten.

6.1 Quality assessment

It is therefore fitting that at this stage a short description should be given of methods used in the assessment of food qualities by organoleptic methods. These may vary from the simple cooking of the food products and their tasting by a few cooks or laboratory workers to elaborate, statistically controlled, examinations in specially designed rooms. In these rooms each examiner, who has been carefully tested for his or her powers of discrimination and consistency, is placed in a separate small room or division of a main one, the lighting is controlled and odours from the kitchens eliminated. Each examiner produces a report based on a score sheet, assessing the characteristics under examination numerically. The usual characteristics are colour, flavour, texture and sometimes odour. Many variations are possible depending on the characteristics of the food under examination. For taste-panels evaluating the products of research and development trials the results are presented in such a manner that statistical evaluation of the significance of difference is possible.

In taste-panel work the worker is first statistically tested to ensure, so far as possible, that he is an efficient, unemotional instrument. It is fitting perhaps to contrast this with Brillat-Savarin's* test of the effect of the dish of food on the consumer:

> 'Whenever a dish of known and very special flavour shall be set upon the board, the guests shall be closely scrutinised and those whose countenance proclaims no rapture shall be marked down as unworthy.'

6.2 Nutritional values

It is as well to point out at once that no form of food treatment increases the nutritional value of the raw food. However, losses of some nutrients

* Brillat-Savarin, J. A. (1755–1826), *The Physiology of Taste*, 1960 translation. Dover Publications Inc., New York.

begin with harvesting or slaughter and a processed food will normally be of higher nutritional value after a period of storage than the same food kept 'fresh' over a much shorter storage period.

In addition to water and oxygen the following are essential for life and health:

Carbohydrates	sources of energy (including heat), they also may be readily converted into fats and oils in the body
Fats	supply energy (especially heat) and also body fat
Proteins	supply the material for growth and repair of body tissues, may also provide energy
Minerals	necessary for various metabolic processes and also for growth and repair
Vitamins and other substances normally present in very small amounts	necessary for the regulation of body processes

Carbohydrates, fats and proteins when absorbed by the body supply the energy for the maintenance of body temperature and for anabolic processes. The amounts of energy available per gramme are:

Carbohydrates (as glucose)	15.6 kJ (3.75 kcal)*
Fat	38.9 kJ (9.3 kcal)
Protein	17.1 kJ (4.1 kcal)

* 1 kcal = 4.18 kJ *Note.* The figures given above are those generally accepted in the literature of nutrition but a Committee of the Royal Society has recently recommended the following factors: carbohydrate (as monosaccharide) 16 kJ/g, fat 37 kJ/g and protein 17 kJ/g (Royal Society, 1972).

Insufficient supplies of any of the nutrients cause malnutrition, and severe shortages starvation. Over-eating can also lead to forms of malnutrition, e.g. obesity.

6.3   Food composition tables

The amount of energy and of each nutrient obtained by the body for any quantity of foods may be calculated from Food Composition Tables. These usually supply figures for each food prepared in the various ways in which it may be eaten. For the diets of the United Kingdom the tables of MCCANCE & WIDDOWSON (1967) are normally used.

Table 3 Recommended intakes (per person per day) (based on the Department of Health and Social Security's Recommendations, 1969)

Category	Protein g	Thiamine mg	Riboflavine mg	Nicotinic acid equivalents mg	Vitamin C mg	Vitamin A* µg	Vitamin D* µg	Calcium mg	Iron mg
Man									
over 65	56	0.9	1.7	18	30	750	2.5	500	10
sedentary	66	1.1	1.7	18	30	750	2.5	500	10
active	74	1.2	1.7	18	30	750	2.5	500	10
Woman									
over 60	50	0.8	1.3	15	30	750	2.5	500	10
sedentary	55	0.9	1.3	15	30	750	2.5	500	12
active	63	1.0	1.3	15	30	750	2.5	500	12
pregnancy (latter part)	60	1.0	1.6	18	60	750	10	1200	15
Child									
under 1 year	20	0.3	0.4	5	15	450	10	600	6
5–6 years	45	0.7	0.9	10	20	300	2.5	500	8
10–12 years	61	1.0	1.3	15	25	625	2.5	700	13
Boy									
15 years	75	1.2	1.6	18	30	750	2.5	600	15
18–20 years	75	1.2	1.7	18	30	750	2.5	500	10
Girl									
15 years	58	0.9	1.4	16	30	750	2.5	600	15
18–20 years	55	0.9	1.3	15	30	750	2.5	500	12

*Vitamin A is expressed as retinol equivalents and vitamin D as cholecalciferol (1 IU vitamin D = 0.025 µg cholecalciferol).

6.4   Nutritional requirements

Nutritional needs in terms of energy and specific nutrients vary with sex, age and activity as well as with less well defined characteristics such as state of health.

In spite of the evident difficulties tables have been compiled for use in different countries of recommended intakes of each nutrient for various groups of people. In the United Kingdom the Department of Health and Social Security's 'Recommended Intakes of Nutrients for the United Kingdom (1969)' are used in calculating the nutritional well-being of the population.

The energy requirement of a man over 65 years old is given as 9405 kJ while a very active younger man is estimated to need 15048 kJ per day. Women have somewhat lesser needs, e.g. energy requirements of (1) woman over 60, 8360 kJ, (2) active woman, 10450 kJ, (3) woman in latter part of pregnancy, 10032 kJ.

Other examples are given in Table 3.

Good health is based on a well balanced diet which may be obtained in many ways. However, even allowing for difference in tastes and local habits it is possible to devise adequate diets based on the recommended nutrient allowances and the foods locally available. To the extent to which local diets fall short of these recommended allowances (which are estimates of requirements) then mal- or under-nutrition will occur.

6.5   Food processing and nutritive values

The treatments used in food processing are physical, chemical or mechanical or combinations of these. They were summarized in Chapter 1.

Britain imports about half of its food supplies and of that which is home-produced most is eaten at a distance from its place of production and frequently in a different season. Accordingly one or more of the treatments described earlier is necessary to preserve the food and to present it in an edible and attractive form.

Most treatments affect the nutritive values of foods usually by greater or lesser destruction of individual nutrients. But to summarize very briefly, the final result of storage and processing is greatly to increase the supplies of nutrients to the population. Whatever adverse opinions may be expressed on various methods both of food production and subsequent treatments it should be borne in mind that the British public is much better nourished now than it was in the 'pre-technological' age.

It is not possible in a small book to cover the effects of all the processes given to foods but illustrations may be taken from, the milling and baking industries, which include grinding and heating treatments.

All cereal-based foods in the U.K. diet contribute about 30% of the energy intake of the population while bread and flour contribute nearly

20%. The contributions of these products in terms of individual nutrients are shown in Table 4 (National Food Survey, 1968).

Table 4   Intake of nutrients—All households—1968. (Expressed as % of total intake)

	All cereal-based products	Bread and flour
Protein	27.6	21.0
Calcium	23.7	17.7
Iron	30.8	21.0
Vitamin B_1	33.4	24.6
Nicotinic Acid	26.0	17.6

Eleven to twelve per cent of the energy provided by the national diet as a whole comes from protein. The average protein energy content of bread is just over 13% and since rather more than one-fifth of the population's protein supply comes from bread and flour then about 2–3% of the total protein energy supply is from bread which makes it a valuable source of protein.

During *milling* some losses of nutrients occur and some of these are required by law to be made up to the level obtaining in 80% extraction flour. This extraction rate is the one adopted during the War based on nutritional experience and acceptability. Present day white flour (70% or lower extraction) is supplemented by additions of vitamin B_1, nicotinic acid and iron. Calcium is also added at present to ensure an adequate supply in the diet but the need for this is still debated.

Canning, in which foods may be subjected to considerable heat treatments, is a process where losses of nutrients may be expected. However with modern methods these losses can be small. In particular with aseptic canning, losses are small or non-existent for thiamine and pyridoxine. With conventional methods of canning there may be appreciable losses; up to 40% of thiamine in canned vegetables and losses of biological value of proteins in meat. Fish appears to be able to withstand quite severe heat treatment without great loss of nutritional quality.

The ultra-high temperature (UHT) *sterilizing treatment of milk* consists of heating for not less than 1 sec at a temperature of at least 135 °C followed by filling into containers under aseptic conditions. This relatively new development gives rise to little or no greater nutritional loss than that caused by the now conventional HTST (high temperature short time) pasteurizing treatment of milk although somewhat higher losses of vitamin B_6 and vitamin B_{12} have been reported. UHT processing appears to have little effect on milk proteins except for some destruction of the lacto-globulins. Some loss of total free fatty acids is said to occur.

No *irradiated* foods have yet been approved in the U.K. for public sale and human consumption with the one exception that permission has been granted to use irradiated diets for certain hospital patients requiring sterilized foods. However, the possibilities are considerable and the method of such current interest that mention of its effects on nutritive values is desirable. Relatively low dose treatments of food (up to 1 Mrad) produce generally quite small changes in nutritive value. Changes at high doses (5–6 Mrad) are about the same as occur in conventional procedures such as canning and cooking, some destruction of pyridoxine and ascorbic acid may occur and thiamine is relatively rather more sensitive. Except at high dose levels there is little effect on carbohydrates but oxidation of some fats may occur.

Convenience foods are foods which need minimal domestic or catering processing. Their production and use has increased rapidly in the past ten or so years. Lack of information on the effects on nutritive values in their production leads to difficulties in assessing the nutritional value of individual and national diets since available food composition tables include but few of recent products. However, there are indications that revision of such works as 'Composition of Foods' (McCance & Widdowson, 1967) is planned. While there is no reason at present to believe that supplies of nutrients are decreasing due to increasing and varied forms of processing it is desirable that there should be adequate confirmation of this belief.

The latest development in meat simulators appear to be adequate nutritionally. Texturized vegetable proteins resembling meat are found to have proteins of somewhat lower biological value than meat protein but the vitamin and iron contents are similar.

6.6 General

To sum up: it appears that present methods of food production and food processing do not adversely affect the nutritional value of food to any substantial extent. Much more food gets to many more people than it could without the application of modern technology. But for the food scientist and nutritionist to remain reasonably confident it is important that the nutrient content of a new or altered food product be examined as soon as possible after development so that an assessment can be made of its nutritional implications. Advancing technology has enabled not only new processing methods to be developed but also entirely new products to be formulated.

There is increasing need for close collaboration between those creating the new technological applications and nutritionists (and dietitians) so that the effects of change may be foreseen and assessed.

7 Looking to the Future

The future in relation to the food supply of the United Kingdom, which imports approximately 50% of its food does not, at first, appear promising. World population is increasing rapidly, world food production *per capita* is decreasing, so food production surpluses tend to be less available to importing countries. The U.K. traditionally has filled the gap between its food demands and its food production by exporting manufactured goods. The demand for these may not increase and may decrease as other countries increase their competition.

In the short run, the main problems of food supply in the U.K. are likely to be related to costs. The raw materials of the food industries both home produced and imported will, almost certainly, cost more. Costs of labour and equipment in food factories, and of transport of both raw materials and of end products, are rising. The days of deliveries from shops to consumers appear rapidly to be coming to an end due to both the expense of the operation, and to the increasing use by families of the car to collect a week's supply, or more, from supermarkets and to store them till needed, using deep-freezes for perishables.

Another tendency is for less food preparation to be done in the home and more at the factory. The relatively expensive convenience foods are used more and more as employment of women outside the home increases.

These economic and sociological factors combined will lead biologists, and others, to search for new more efficient methods of using the earth's crops, and new methods of producing foods.

Biologists already work in different parts of the food industries, particularly in those concerned with milk and milk products, meat and fish products and with beer, wines and spirits. But with newer developments for the substitution of vegetable protein foods for animal products, the need for biologists, including biochemists, will undoubtedly increase.

The meat simulants now being developed from vegetable crops (soya, groundnuts, field beans, etc.,) fungi (particularly food yeast) and bacteria (some using hydrocarbons as substrates) demand research by scientists trained in many disciplines mainly biological (biochemists, mycologists, bacteriologists). With increasing development and expansion into large scale production control scientists with considerable biological training will evidently be needed.

It is no idle dream that these new types of foods can be produced, and produced in sufficient quantity in the near future to make an impact on supplies of high-protein foods, but their presentation may well give rise to problems. It is in this area that the practical type of scientific worker may be involved. Domestic science workers and dietitians will be needed to develop palatable dishes and advise on their nutritive values.

These developments will not solve the world's overall shortages but can alleviate local shortages of expensive high-protein meat and fish supplies. It is likely that cost and prejudices will be the main factors operating at first against the acceptance of such new foods though increasing experience of them and developments in their presentation in attractive forms will assist their acceptance.

The simulated meat products appear today as new types of food, though they have been under development for some years. The use of algae to produce food has not developed very far, but may well become more attractive if more effort is given to research and development. The ultimate aim of producing virtually unlimited supplies of food must lie in the distant future. However, it is by no means impossible that if groups of biological, physical and chemical research workers, concentrate on the problems underlying the production of carbohydrates and proteins from the constituents of the earth's atmosphere and crust, food may be truly synthesized. Already, it is possible to synthesize amino acids and build from them simple proteins. Reduction of the small amounts of carbon dioxide in the atmosphere would need great amounts of energy to produce carbohydrates in any quantity but there may be possibilities from nuclear and particularly nuclear fusion energy.

These projections into the future may seem esoteric but progress in other areas of research and development, e.g. production and utilization of nuclear energy, have been commensurate with the suggested possibilities in a remarkably short space of time. It may well be that in the near distance there will be difficulties in terms of supply and price of foods for the consumer and manufacturer in the U.K., but there is no reason to be pessimistic about long term expectations given the continued and expanding application of science and technology to the problems.

The development of new foods, and the ultimate goal of food synthesis from the atmosphere, at present employ the activities of relatively few biologists but more immediate problems employ increasing numbers.

The attainment of a marketable food product requires that it be 'wholesome', of attractive appearance, have the flavour characteristic of the product and the colour and texture appropriate to the food. The ultimate objective in both the storing and processing of food is to retain, so far as possible, the elusive bloom of fresh foods. Behind this objective there lies much biological research and control work in hygiene, infestation control and microbiological control.

Perhaps, so far there has been more technological than biological development apparent in the food industries. However, there is now more effort on the biological problems relating to quality; appearance, flavour, texture and microbiological quality. There are also parallel and increasing efforts to deal with problems of waste treatment and pollution.

References and Further Reading

References

BARNELL, H. R. and HOLLINGSWORTH, D. F. (1956). *Proc. Nutr. Soc.*, **15**, 142.

BUNKER, H. J. (1966). *2nd Int. Congr. Food Sci. & Techn.*, Warsaw.

DEPT. OF HEALTH AND SOC. SEC. (1969). *Rpts. on Public Health and Med. Subs.*, No. 120, H.M.S.O.

LEA, D. E. (1955). *Actions of Radiations on Living Cells*, 2nd edition. Cambridge University Press.

MCCANCE, R. A. and WIDDOWSON, E. M. (1967). M.R.C. Special Report Series, No. 297. H.M.S.O.

MIN. OF HEALTH (1964). Comm. on Med. & Nutr. Aspects of Food Policy. Rept. of Working Party on the Irradiation of Food. H.M.S.O.

MIN. OF AGRIC. FISH AND FOOD (1961). *The Accelerated Freeze-drying Method of Food Preservation*. H.M.S.O.

STOKES, J. L. (1968). *Nature of Physchrophilic Organisms in Low Temp. Biol. of Foods*. Ed. Hawthorne, J. and Rolfe, E. Pergamon Press, Oxford.

NATIONAL FOOD SURVEY COMMITTEE. *Annual Report for 1968*. H.M.S.O., 1970.

Further Reading

AUSTIN, C. (1968). *The Science of Wine*. Univ. of London Press.

BENDER, A. E. (1968). *Dictionary of Nutrition and Food Technology* (3rd ed.). Butterworth, London.

BRAVERMAN, J. B. S. (1963). *Introduction to the Biochemistry of Foods*. Elsevier, Amsterdam.

DAVIES, J. G. (1967). Fundamentals of Dairy Chemistry, *Chem. Ind.* (4), 1675–8.

DRUMMOND, J. C. and WILBRAHAM, A. (1958). *The Englishman's Food*. Cape, London.

DUCKWORTH, R. B. (1966). *Fruit and Vegetables*. Pergamon Press, Oxford.

HAWTHORNE, J. and ROLFE, E. J. (1969). *Low Temperature Biology of Foodstuffs*. Pergamon Press, Oxford.

HILL, F. (1967). Quality in Meat and Quality Control of Meat Products. *Fd. Mg.*, **42** (11), 38–41 and 51.

HOBBS, B. (1968). *Food Poisoning and Food Hygiene* (2nd ed.). Edward Arnold, London.

KENT–JONES, D. W. and AMOS, A. J. (1967). *Modern Cereal Chemistry* (6th ed.). North. Pub. Co., Liverpool.

LAWRIE, R. A. (1966). *Meat Science*. Pergamon Press, Oxford.

LAWRIE, R. A. (1968). Chemical Changes in Meat due to Processing: a review. *J. Sci. Fd. Agric.*, **19** (5), 233–40.

MINNIFIE, B. W. (1970). *Chocolate, Cocoa & Confectionery; Science & Technology*, J. & A. Churchill, London.

POTTER, N. W. (1968). *Food Science*. AVI, Westport, Conn.

SMITH, D. E. and WALTERS, A. H. (1967). *Introductory Food Science*. Classic Publications, London.

The Information Division of Unilever Ltd. publish an interesting and useful series of booklets on specialized subjects of which the following is a selection:

Food Preservation, The Chemistry of Proteins, The Chemistry of Glycerides, Margarine and Cooking Fats, Vegetable Oils and Fats, Water